A
Monmouthshire
Christmas

A Monmouthshire Christmas

Compiled by Maria & Andrew Hubert

ALAN SUTTON PUBLISHING LIMITED

First published in the United Kingdom in 1995
Alan Sutton Publishing Limited · Phoenix Mill · Far Thrupp
Stroud · Gloucestershire

Copyright © this compilation, Maria and Andrew Hubert, 1995

Ten per cent of the authors' royalty is going towards the
maintenance of St Mary's Catholic Church in Monmouth, the
oldest post-Reformation Catholic parish church in Wales.

All rights reserved. No part of this publication may be
reproduced, stored in a retrieval system, or transmitted, in
any form or by any means, electronic, mechanical,
photocopying, recording or otherwise, without the prior
permission of the publishers and copyright holders.

British Library Cataloguing in Publication Data.

A catalogue record for this book is available from the
British Library.

ISBN 0-7509-1081-X

Cover illustration: 1860s Christmas card, based on a Cole-
Horsely design of 1842.

Typeset in Garamond 12/13.
Typesetting and origination by
Alan Sutton Publishing Limited.
Printed in Great Britain by
Ebenezer Baylis, Worcester.

*To the noble Welshmen of Gwent and the worthy
Englishmen of Monmouthshire and its borderland
neighbours, who care enough about Monmouthshire
Christmas to share their memories — and to all those
whose memories we could have included given time and
a bigger book!*

Contents

A Monmouthshire Christmas

Christmas in Gwent

ANON

*This poem was donated to the Christmas Archives when
Monmouthshire became Gwent in 1975.*

From my window, a frosty wonderland,
All dressed up for its Christmas stand.
This mysterious corner
Ancient Archenfeld straddled border to border.
Doward and Dixton, where shires met,
Wales and Gloucester, Hereford and Gwent.

Vortigern fought here, Claudia prayed,
Generations of Farmers and Miners have stayed.
Did Dubricius crown Arthur
At Usk Christmas Day?
And was Thackeray inspired
Along the Wye Way?

Hoar frost's mantle covers landscape with rime,
It's a Wye Valley Christmas caught in time.
A place which attracts
An escape from the city,
Mist low on the river
And Christmas card pretty.

In ancient stone dwellings are ovens galore
To tell of a time in days of past lore

1

Hoar frost deep in the
Monmouthshire countryside.

When each villager staggered
With cakes, pies and meat
To the bakery ovens
To cook Christmas treats.

First stop outside Wales, first place for a beer,
Brought charabancs queuing – Christmas Day's here!
The big houses visited,
Carols were sung
At granges and manors
'Til Christmas bells rung.

On hillside and valley, by river and dell
Old folk will remember, as tales weave their spell.
Before memories fade
And old customs are spent.
On a hoar frosty morn
Think of Christmas in Gwent.

William de Braose's Christmas Surprise

There were uneasy relationships along the Welsh/English border in twelfth-century Monmouthshire. One lord was friendly to his Welsh neighbours, another hostile, as the lands of the ancient Kingdom of Gwent were divided between Norman knights and Welsh princes. But mostly they kept an uneasy peace.

After the Norman Conquest many of the Welsh princes had their lands seized, but one prince, Dyfnwal, was allowed to retain his manors, his lands and his castle. He claimed descent from Ynyr, King of Gwent, and Castell Arnallt was the site of the ancient court of Gwent. His son and heir was Seisyllt, who in 1173 joined forces with other Gwent princes from Caerleon and Chepstow to attack Abergavenny, which was held by a Norman lord, Henry FitzMilo, whom he killed. Seisyllt held Abergavenny for a few years, before being persuaded by his father-in-law, Lord Rhys, to make peace; this he did, Abergavenny going in 1175 to a nephew of Henry FitzMilo, William de Braose. William accepted his inheritance quietly, perhaps, so people thought, because he was pleased to inherit the castle and its lands, so he had turned a blind eye to the injustice of his uncle's murder.

As Christmas 1176 approached, William sent out invitations to his Welsh neighbours for the Christmas feast. All Seisyllt's knights and entourage came, his elder son, Gruffyd, and other Welsh princes and chieftains – some

seventy men in all. This was seen as a gesture of friendship, to strengthen the bonds between the new lord of Abergavenny and his neighbour who had, apparently, abused that bond by the murder of Henry.

As was the custom, all weapons were left at the door of the Great Hall. They probably made the usual obeisance under the sacramental Holy Bough to show there was no enmity in their hearts at this Christmastide, and they sat side by side, de Braose's men and Seisyllt's men, under the benevolent gaze of the genial host, William.

During the meal, William suddenly made what he claimed was a royal ordinance, a request that all the Welsh leaders present should take an oath promising that they would henceforth travel unarmed through Gwent. Naturally the Welsh objected most strongly, as it was not safe in those days to travel unarmed.

Then, at a sign, the great doors were locked and guarded. De Braose's men drew hidden daggers, and massacred every one of the unarmed Welsh knights.

Not satisfied with his bloody and sacrilegious action, de Braose followed it up by sending men to Seisyllt's home, Castell Arnallt, to wreak havoc there too, killing Seisyllt's small son, Cadwaladr, and taking his wife prisoner.

The Welsh had their revenge several years later, laying seige to Abergavenny Castle in 1182; but de Braose's cruelty was never forgotten, and the continual retaliation between subsequent generations of English and Welsh lords made the Borders a highly volatile area for many years, with accusations and skirmishes breaking out at the slightest provocation. One such incident involves William de Broase's grandson, also of the same name, who was accused and hanged by the Welsh for seducing the wife of the great warrior prince Llewelyn, an act intended merely to prove superiority over the Welsh.

The Calennig

Being a much disputed border area, Monmouthshire has been part of England and part of Wales, and thus maintains customs from both countries. The Calennig is one of the Welsh customs which are peculiar to Monmouthshire.

The name 'Calennig' comes from the Latin 'Kalends', which was the name for the New Year festival in Roman times. Some say that this custom has come down unaltered for two thousand years, and it is certainly possible. The Romans gave each other branches of olive from the sacred groves of their goddess of health, Strenia, as a way of wishing someone good health for the coming year. In Wales, including Monmouthshire, which was densely occupied by the Romans, children carry round apples usually stuck with cloves, sticks, sprays of evergreen, nuts and other such bits. At each house they visit, they sing a little song and prepare the offering. The sticks form a sort of tripod stand, the spray is attached to the top and nuts are sometimes hung from it. The children hope to get something in return for their singing; these days it is usually money, or a few sweets: in times past, it could be food for their families. The songs vary along the border. In Newport and close to Cardiff they sing:

> I come out of my house today
> With a bag and sticks with me
> My task to give my gift
> And to fill my bag with bread and cheese.

The Calennig – ancient and modern. Left: the traditional apple on a tripod stand, studded with evergreens and cloves; right: a modern Calennig, in some areas called a 'Christingle', given as a good luck token.

At Chepstow the Calennig is usually called a 'Monty', though it is only a memory today. Some people say that the term 'Monty' is a corruption of 'Morning to ye'. There they sang:

Monty, Monty, Happy New Year
A pocket full of money and a cellar full of beer.

Few children go around singing now, alas, but the apple on its tripod survives as a decoration in many homes, particularly in east Monmouthshire.

Fred Hando, prolific Monmouthshire writer, recounts how he first encountered the Calennig between the wars: 'The people of the moorland keep green the rites and customs of their

forefathers. In a village inn, early in January, I saw on the mantlepiece a bright apple standing on three silvered twigs, and surmounted by a sprig of box. The boys of the village had taken it to the inn, "to see the New Year in", and had been rewarded with a new threepenny piece. It was a Calennig.'

Arthur Machin, fellow Monmouthshireman and journalist, recounts his memories of the custom in his book *The Pleasant Land of Gwent* (1944): 'When I was a boy in Caerleon-on-Usk the town children got the biggest and bravest and gayest apple they could find in the loft, deep in the dry bracken. They put bits of gold leaf upon it. They stuck raisins into it. They inserted into the apple little sprigs of box, and then they delicately slit the ends of hazelnuts, and so worked that the nuts appeared to grow from the ends of the holly leaves. . . . At last, three bits of stick were fixed into the base of the apple, tripod-wise; and so it was borne round from house to house; and the children got cakes and sweets, and those were wild days, remember – small cups of ale.'

He then traces the Calennig to the Roman Saturnalia, and suggests that the custom was brought to Caerleon by the Romans: 'My own view is that the Calennig, like the White Horse on our southern hills, was a symbol used in the ritual of the ancient fertility cults, long before the Romans came. On the first blackout New Year's Eve of the war I arrived home at midnight to find in the light of my flashlamp a very gay Calennig resting on my doorstep. An orange, supported by three silvered sticks, held up by a large spray of holly, and on every spine of the holly leaves raisins had been transfixed. This delightful gift had been left by a lady who remembered the customs from her childhood days in Chepstow, and who informed me that I must not remove the orange until it was quite withered, whereupon I should see a happy year. I followed her instructions. I saw my happy year. May such a charming custom never die!'

The Mari Lwyd

This was another custom which all but died out but was kept alive into living memory at Caerleon until well after the First World War. The custom enjoyed a brief revival, courtesy of the Caerleon Local History Society, in the 1960s, but is rarely seen in these parts today. It has its roots firmly in pagan Celtic tradition, similar customs appearing in other parts of Britain and in Europe, and was quite grisly. A horse's skull was specially boiled and prepared, decorated with ribbons and had a stick attached to its lower jaw so that the carrier, who was covered by a white sheet, could 'snap' the jaws. The following accounts explain and describe the custom in more detail. Here is an account, taken in 1980, of a vicar's daughter who grew up in Monmouthshire, in which she remembers, not so fondly, the Mari Lwyd Christmas of 1908.

'I remember one Christmas in particular, I was sixteen, and had long skirts and my hair up for the first time. I was allowed to stay up after dinner with the grown-ups too. It was a very special year. Father stayed long enough to smoke a cigar – a Christmas treat mother allowed the men without them having to leave the room. Then he closeted himself in his study to prepare his sermons for the next day. However, when the men came with the Mari Lwyd, I could not bring myself to stay, and scuttled upstairs to hide! It was quite alarming, and had always frightened we children. A grisly horse's skull, covered in a sheet under which a man hid, working the great snapping jaws.

'The idea was that the horse and its entourage should chase through the house, chasing out all the evil spirits with it. But we lived right up the hill, and by the time they got to us it was very late, and the men had had a lot to drink, so they were loud, shouting and laughing a lot, and not beyond slapping and pinching the maids if they were caught. It was considered bad luck not to let them enter, and although Father did not believe in such superstitions, being a man of the cloth, he nevertheless could not refuse to admit these men from his parish without causing much ill-feeling, so we had to endure it. There was a custom involved whereby the Mari Lwyd entourage would sing a couplet, and we had to answer with the right verse in return. Mother made sure that the menservants could do this, otherwise she would have been obliged to feed them all with as much food and drink as they wanted, which would have emptied the larder for sure!

'As it was they were given refreshments, though my father made sure that the ale was weak, the weakness disguised with spice and heated up, and served with big soft breadcakes, well fruited and spread with butter. Father would then shoo them out with the excuse that the household had to be up earlier than most, and the evening was over.'

Dr Roy Saer of the Museum of Welsh Life has done much work on the folk songs and carols of the Welsh countryside. It is from his writings that we have learnt much about the mystery of the Mari Lwyd songs. The group would arrive and sing traditional stanzas at the house door, which issued a versifying challenge to the household. The Mari Lwyd could outverse and outquip them all, and if it did, then entry must be admitted and food and drink given. As the following song says, they were prepared to stay all night if necessary in this musical combat of wits. These were in turn responded to by someone within, and what ensued was a lot of leg-pulling, heavy humour, mock insults, etc. This repartee was called the 'pwnco'.

The Mari Lwyd entourage visiting Llanover Hall. Lady Llanover
kept alive many of the old Welsh customs. This nineteenth-century
painting now hangs over the post office in Llanover village.

Once the first part was won, and the entourage had access to the house, they would perform very much as the mummers in other parts of Britain did. Each member of the group would be introduced, in verse, and then they would perform and entertain until the cakes and ale were brought. Thus replete, a farewell was sung with all good wishes all round. The Caerleon group consisted of Merryman, who played the music and did tricks; Sergeant, who supposedly kept everyone in order; and Judy, who swept the hearth, symbolic of the sweeping out of the evil spirits of ancient times. Punch provided the slapstick pantomime with Judy, hitting her, then kissing all the ladies present and being chased from room to room by Judy and her broom.

Here follows a translation of one of the versions, showing the repartee which went on between the Mari Lwyd group and the

The Pentyrch Mari Lwyd.

household. Many versions are the same but for the odd word-change here and there in some stanzas, an obvious result of oral tradition.

Mari Lwyd: Behold, here we come simple friends, to ask permission to sing.

House: Let us hear, wise men, how many of you are there and what exactly are your names?

ML: Six fine men, the best in the world, to sing truly for ale.

H: Let us hear, honest men, where you come from, and what is your request if I may ask?

ML: The fashion of wassailing has existed for a thousand years, and in set forms as I shall prove.

H: I rose from my bed being fully determined to win against you.

ML: Sing your best, I shall do so too, and whoever is the best shall have ale.

H: It is no use your pushing us to lift the latch tonight, since I am an unbeatable rhymer.

The Mari Lwyd at Llangynwyd.

ML: My talent is aroused as I think of singing at night in bed.
H: Away with you thieves, go away at once, you shall not cheerfully see me!
ML: I'll sing for a week, a fortnight even or a month, if need be – there's a challenge to you.
H: I'll sing for a year, if God is beside me, without fearing any evening during the holidays.
ML: Oh, tap the barrel, let it flow freely, don't be too stingy with singers.
H: Jenkins the parson is coming, upon my soul he will make you leave my dwelling.
ML: Merry Mari Lwyd wants to come to your house, and to sing is her purpose, I believe.

Once the Mari Lwyd is allowed in there ensues another round of verses sung by the Mari Lwyd whilst the entourage dances, plays and generally buffoons around, sometimes, as in Caerleon, sweeping the floor through to the door. The singer introduces all the characters in the group in a similar way to the mummers' plays in England, and in flowery terms describes the Wassail Bowl.

The Fair Folk [fairies] of the household come to the light without hiding, to see the Wassail without pain, there's not one like it in Wales.

It is an orchard of broad flowers beautiful indeed and liveried, marvellously speckled ribbons have been tied into bows.

It is a nimble comely Mare, thousands praise her, her head is decorated with knotted strips.

Fine Sergeant and his company will boldly lead us, there is also a sprightly Corporal for this work.

13

The Ostler will lead his Mare in, bringing his bridle and saddle with him to run about the place.

Punch and Judy who are kindred spirits will also come – two rogues as black as sin or hell itself.

Now I shall cease singing, give me something to eat. A Happy New Year to you all, and to everybody in the world for that matter.

A lovely story which crops up again and again when talking to the folk of Caerleon, and is famous enough to have been written up by a number of highly respected Monmouthshire local historians, is that of the Mari Lwyd and the Bulldog.

The custom of Mari Lwyd lasted well into the thirties; by then no one knew what the Welsh words meant, but they sang them anyway, and they particularly liked to have a go at the foreigners coming to live in the area. It must have been a few years before the war when an English family settled at Glanusk. They had been told that the Mari Lwyd would pay them a visit, with great detail applied to the description of the horse and the customs. This family, whether from bad sportsmanship or sheer fright, decided that they would avoid this particular tradition! They had a big fierce bulldog, which on the night of the Mari Lwyd they put out to guard their gate. The group came, the dog barked and growled – the Mari Lwyd clacked its jaws in the poor dog's face, and it, never having seen anything the like before, ran yelping to safety!

However, although they had won the first round of the game of entry, the Mari Lwyd party were quite insulted about this snub from the English family, and went to the Bull Public House to drink away their chagrin!

Plygain

*Plygain is one of the most beautiful customs to come out of Wales
and be adopted by the Border country.*

Midnight Mass was originally celebrated at cockcrow – and so
was called Cockcrow Mass. Before the Reformation, 'Plygain'
was the term formally used to denote this early morning
service, which was not a specifically Christmas service as now.
When attending Mass was banned under the Commonwealth
rule of Oliver Cromwell's parliament, the menfolk would go
out still at cockcrow, and have a sort of impromptu Christmas
sing-song. Little was written down: this was an oral tradition,
as are many of the Welsh traditions. Certain songs, made up
by one person, would be passed from father to son, and are
still today associated with individual families.

The songs could be religious or secular; there were also
verse and prose recitations. There was often no musical
accompaniment other than the polyphonic harmonies of the
men's voices, a stirring event indeed. The carols were written
in traditional metres, and set to old folktunes from both
England and Wales, made popular in the areas by the old
Welsh ballad singers. Being already familiar with the tunes
made it easier for the singers to memorize the often epic
verses written by the poets for the occasion.

Modified from the pre-Reformation Catholic service to
meet Protestant requirements, the Plygain survived into the
nineteenth century where it met with another religious
upheaval, Nonconformism. In many areas this meant the

complete demise of the Plygain, but South Wales and
Monmouthshire held out, and Plygain became one of the very
few traditional church festivals not discarded by the chapels,
the character of the custom modifying yet again to the new
Nonconformity rules. There are places, however, particularly
in Monmouthshire, where it remained unchanged into living
memory.

Accounts from the areas of Monmouthshire with most
Welsh influence show that, within living memory, the
Plygain service was well attended. The services were held
between 3 a.m. and 6 a.m. For places where early service was
observed, many people passed the night either in groups carol
singing door to door – even the Mari Lwyd visited on this
night – or in more homely activities such as toffee-making,
cake-baking and decorating the houses. One old man
remembered sitting at his grandfather's feet half asleep,
listening to the storytelling which went on around the fireside
of his parents' farm, in the Honddu Valley, where the local
menfolk gathered before going on to the chapel for the
singing. He remembered too that his mother and her
neighbours would make many coloured candles, putting
vegetable dyes into the melted waxes and how he and his
sister used to tie old pyjama cords to a pole to make strong
wicks which would be lowered across the candle moulds.

The singers would carry their candles from their homes to
the chapel, and the chapels must have been very cheerful,
with dozens of large coloured candles for illumination, many
decorated further with relief wax patterns and ribbon
streamers. This custom of outdoing the next person by
producing a more elaborately decorated candle seems to be
fairly consistent, while other customs varied depending on the
community and area. Certainly, the brilliant illumination and
the standard of the lights appears to be the most lasting
memory of all those who have left accounts of Plygain.

In the Glamorgan villages, many bordering on to Monmouthshire – Machen, Tredegar, Brynmawr – between two and three hundred candles were used to illuminate the chapels: along the rails, the windowsills, communion tables and pews. In some places the candles were made by the village chandler, particularly at Llanfyllin over the border, and were called 'Canhwyllau plygain'. They had particularly large wicks to withstand sudden gusts of wind and inclement weather on the way to chapel. One person remembers his father putting a little horn 'shade' around the flame, which he would make by scouring out the inside layers of an ox horn until it was thin enough to let some light through.

Plygain Parti Llanfihangel; carol singing at Llanfihangel-yng-Ngwynfa Church, Powys. Photo: Tegwyn Roberts.

A Monmouthshire Christmas

*An old account by a William Payne from the middle of the
nineteenth century provides a vivid description of a Plygain.*

Now the Church is in a blaze, now crammed body, aisle and
gallery, now Siôn Roberts, the club-footed shoemaker, and his
wife, descending from the singing seat to the lower and front
part of the gallery, strike up alternatively, and without
artificial aid of pitch-pipe, the long, long carol and old
favourite describing the Worship of the Kings and of the
Wise Men, and the Flight into Egypt, and the terrible
wickedness of Herod. The crowds are wholly silent and rapt in
admiration. Then the good rector, and his curate, David
Pugh, stand up, and read the morning service abbreviated,
finishing with the prayer for All Conditions of Men, and the
Benediction – restless and somewhat surging is the congregation
during prayers – the Rector obliged sometimes to stop short
in his office and look direct at some part or persons, but no
verbal admonishment.

Prayers over, the singers begin again more carols, new
singers, old carols in solos, duets, trios, choruses, then silence
in the audience, broken at the appropriate times by the
suppressed hum of delight and approval, till between eight
and nine, hunger telling on the singers, the Plygain is over,
and the bells strike out a round peal.

The custom ceased towards the end of the nineteenth
century, although in some cases, as we have seen, it lasted a
little longer. In some areas it was said that the custom ceased
because of 'disorder on account of men under the influence of
drink attending the church after a night of revelry'.

from

Diary of a Farmer's Wife – 1

MARY ANNE HUGHES

The Diary of a Farmer's Wife *describes life on a large
Monmouthshire farm in the eighteenth century. Its author,
Mary Anne Hughes, as an old lady in her eighties, read from
her diary to a young girl named Jeanne Preston, who wrote it
all down. Jeanne always intended to publish the stories, which
were serialized in the* Farmers Weekly *in the 1930s. Later
the diary was televised, and subsequently published in book
form by Penguin. Anne's entries for December give us a perfect
picture of her Christmas on her husband's farm near Chepstow.
The year is not known, but believed to be in the 1780s. Note
the archaic and inconsistent spelling.*

Dec. ye 19. I have had no time for writing in my book for
sum days. The snow be all gone, and all the roads be deep in
mud, so that we out only on horseback and do put on our
pattens to sweep the yard place.

Carters ladd be off for a soldier and a verrie good thing too
for he will be safe and not trubble his mother any more. Tim
Prew be gone also, it were he who did make Carters ladd
wild.

Farmer Jones did lose many sheep in the snow, and sum pigges have bin drowned in the flood water. I be glad ours are all safe. John do say we on the hill the water do run away from us. It be but 6 days to Christmas, and I do hope the mud will be all gone by then, for John's cusson Tom be cumming, and Emma and her ladd and his sweetheart. We have not heard how Mistress Prue and her sister have fared in the snow but passon did come up on his grey cob to see how we do, and I verrilie believe it was mostly to see Sarah; but he did not, she being at the bed-making.

Later cums John all muddy and water dripping from his britches seat; he slipping up and sat in a great puddel when feeding the pigges. He verrie wroth and did romp about my clene kitchen floor which did vex me sore, but me knowing his temper did go warilie; so up to fetch his dry clothes, the while he out to the pump to wash the mud from his face and out of his hair. He better after a hot drink, out agen, me not daring to laff till he gone, albeit we fit to bust our selfes at John all muddy.

Yet I did laff too soon for me and Sarah out to the pump for a pail of water, down I did go a proper bump in the mud; me catching at Sarah, she down atop of me and the pail falling on her head; and thereat, Johns mother out to see what all the cabbel be about, did laff much at me in the mud with Sarah atop, crowned with a pail.

Sarah laffing much I do beg her to get off me to let me rise, so she up, still laffing, and me up, a sorrie spectacle too, with the muddy water dripping from my gown, and I did hurry in to get rid of it lest John should see and laff last of all.

We soon clean and tidy, and after we to the hemming of the sheets, and John did mend sum harness and divers things, then supper and to bed.

Dec. ye 23. We have bin verrie bussie with sum goodlie things to eat. Boiled hams and great big mince pies and roast

geese and hens and boiled and roasted beef, all reddie for eating. Johns mother be going to make a pudden for Carter and shepherd, and I shall give them a big mince pie and apples, so they can have Christmas fare. Carters wiffe be cumming early to get ready for our visitors who be cumming tomorrow. We shall be verrie bussie, so I shall not have time to write in my book till all over.

Johns mother have made a verrie pretty dish wich she do call meat cake. She did mix flower and butter to a thick paste and put sum on the bottom of a bake tin, this she did cover with the chopt beef and onion and herbs, then more paste, then more meat and flavouring, and paste agen till the tin be full. Then she do cover all with more paste and cook till done. She do say this do cut like a cake when it be cold with the meat inside. There be also 2 roast hares and pudden with spices and plenty of apple pies and divers things and junkets, cider cake and cinnemon cakes and a rich Christmas Cake, Johns mother did bake.

I hope we shall have enough, but I be keeping sum rabbit pies and a big ham ready, in case it be wanted. John will tap the new beer and the honey wine, and we shall have primy rose wine, as well as Eldernberrie, and dandie lyon, so there should be good store.

I do hear John below so must not write more; I do love my little book so do write much and have wrote nearly all the pages, and I dout if I shall start another one, though I do love it.

The Recusants' Christmas

Monmouthshire can boast more than its fair share of saints, martyred for their faith during the religious upheavals of the sixteenth and seventeenth centuries. Religion, it seemed, was no longer God's domain, but the whim of kings and politicians alike in a sanguinous struggle for power which was to last for over a century. Many of the Catholics preferred – either through devoutness or through habit – to stay with the old religion, despite the severe taxes and other penalties which were imposed upon them. Their priests were in most danger, as they were banned from performing their services under pain of an excruciating death by hanging, drawing and quartering. During this period there were moments of respite, moments of renewed hope and moments of bitter despair as one monarch after another took sides, Catholic versus Protestant. Under Cromwell and the Parliamentarians, not only Roman Catholics but the new Anglicans who had conformed to King Henry VIII were persecuted as Monarchists. And so it went on.

In Monmouthshire, as in other areas, Christmas was kept going by the wealthier Catholics who were still able to pay their taxes: the 'greate Christmasses' kept by the Catholic gentry were described by a prominent writer of the day, Richard Carpenter in 1642. Rural areas like Monmouthshire were in a better situation, because it was more difficult for the

Parliamentarian soldiers literally to sniff out the Christmas pies, and the county town of Monmouth itself was strongly Monarchist and Catholic.

Many of the gentry 'kept' a recusant priest. Often a jobbing carpenter, or a tutor for the children, or someone hired to paint portraits of the family, was in fact a priest. Monmouthshire had a number of 'safe houses', where the priests might find safe haven in times of trouble. Houses on the outskirts of Abergavenny, Llangrove and in Monmouth itself had special hidden chambers, often with stairways and chutes leading away from the room for those dangerous moments when the soldiers came searching. In Monmouth there is a secret chapel walled up in the Robin Hood Inn at the bottom of Monnow Street, and a house in St James Square also has a small chamber. (See also the extract 'Abergavenny's Magi' below.)

The great feasts of the Catholic Church, including Christmas, were the times of greatest danger. As the Jesuit saint and recusant martyr John Gerard said, it was at festal times that the pressure on priests' services was most acute, and the chances of their capture highest. The gentry would invite as many known recusants as they dared to attend a party, which would include a secret service held usually in a secret chapel in the house. They could not even trust their servants: no one knew just who was a Parliamentarian 'plant'. The many accounts of captures at Christmas and other festivals bear this out. However, of all the great feasts, Christmas accounts for fewer arrests, perhaps because although it was by far the most important festival of the Catholic year, it still held some of its old 'Goodwill to all men' message for others too. Thus it may have been a general period of truce, or maybe Protestant gentlemen did not wish to be disturbed at this season!

No work was done at Christmas, so both housewives and servants worked twice as hard in the days leading up to the

festival. A priest in the guise of a guest or servant was on hand to do the services of Vespers on Christmas Eve, Confession and the Mass on Christmas Day. This would be followed by Christmas pie, and dancing and card playing. Amongst the lower orders, morris dancing, mumming and noisy games were added to the festivities. There was a strong musical tradition, with plays and songs and much playing of instruments, which was perfectly acceptable at all levels until 1649 when Christmas was officially banned by Parliamentarian edict, and all such things abolished, along with the Christmas pie. Soldiers were paid to spy on households, and sniff the air for the pungent spicy smells of Christmas fare being prepared.

Restrictions were even more tightly adhered to after this date, and the recusant families kept a low profile and a quiet household over Christmas. Perhaps it was merely fear, or maybe the sombre puritanical atmosphere of the times had something to do with it, but the former 'greate Christmasse' – characterized by much jollification and a cheerful daily observance of their religion – gradually became a solemn and spiritual time, the 'merry nights' with friends being observed some time after Christmas Day itself. Diaries of recusants of the times show that Christmas Day was passed in spiritual reading and quiet pastimes, with Mass if they were lucky. By 1700, without the outward excitement and merriment of the festival to keep them going, many of the Catholic community were beginning to see the cycle of fasts, vigils and feasts as an 'irritating hindrance to work'. Christmas weddings were very popular right up to the late seventeenth century, perhaps a way of bringing some legal merriment back into the banned feast of Christmas.

Thus did the priests of Monmouthshire trudge the roads between Abergavenny, the Skirrid Mountain, and Hereford. These old men walked many miles in harsh weather conditions to tend their recusant community, keeping the

Christmas spirit alive in times when all seemed dark with despair. They include John Kemble, whose association with Monmouth is commemorated by a shrine in the oldest Catholic parish church in Wales, St Mary of the Angels in Monmouth, and whose grave in Welsh Newton is a place of pilgrimage still; and David Lewis, born in Abergavenny and caught at Usk in 1679, who is buried in the churchyard of Usk Priory, to which site there is a pilgrimage every year; and others lesser known, who sheltered in the Monmouthshire safe houses, celebrated Christmas with Monmouthshire people and served their flocks all along the Welsh Borderlands.

The Christmas Season at Tredegar House

FROM THE DIARIES AND JOTTINGS OF THE

HOUSE GUESTS

Tredegar House just outside Newport was the family seat of the Viscounts Tredegar. With a medieval wing – the site of the great servants' hall Christmas parties – and Georgian

additions it made a superb setting for the huge seasonal house parties, which began with the November shoots, and ended in mid-January. Here are some of the accounts and diary entries of house guests, housekeepers and journalists of parties in the eighteenth and nineteenth centuries, beginning with an extract from the Memoirs of General Sir Thomas Molyneux (1767–1841).

In December, 1808, we went to spend the Christmas with Sir Charles Morgan at Tredegar in Monmouthshire for the first time. There was an immense large party there consisting of 80 Gentlemen and Ladies, as many servants who were entertained in the Servants Hall, and above 100 horses in this hospitable Baronet's stables.

We continued to pay our annual visits to him every Christmas for the ensuing eight years, generally went there 28th December, the day after my birthday (not wishing to be from home on that, or on Christmas Day) and remained till about the 10th January at which time the party generally dispersed.

1814 – In the December went down to Tredegar to pay our annual visit. A curious scene took place the day after Twelfth Day in January 1815. It was customary to have a masquerade party there on that night, at which I appeared in the character of a Mail Coachman. The next morning I put four of my own horses to Sir Charles Morgan's barouche, and two of Sir William Somerset's for leaders, his servant riding one of them dressed in the full costume of Major Stowegron – myself riding in the dress and mask I appeared in the night before at the Masquerade – and ten or twelve of the characters in the same plight, in and outside the Barouche, that was open.

We then drove into Newport, it being Market day, the concourse of people were immense that gathered round us,

while we stopped to 'malt' at the Kings Head, and as you may well suppose, were not a little astonished when I offered the woman the toll going into the town, she was so frightened at the 'Wonderment' (as she called it) that she ran into the house and would not come out to receive the money either going or on our return to Tredegar!

A note provided by the present curator of Tredegar.

Amongst the most constant of the annual visitors at Tredegar during the six or eight weeks of the Christmas festivities were General and Mrs Milman, with a large family of children, a governess for the girls, and a whole suite of domestics, male and female. The General's town mansion was emptied of its living contents, and left under the sole care of the trusty butler . . . It was an old maxim in military tactics to 'quarter as much as possible upon the enemy'. But when the friendly barracks of Tredegar opened wide its hospitable gates with never failing abundance of loaves, fishes and fleshpots, what need had General Milman to play the marauder?

The season began with small dinner parties and shooting on the private estate of Tredegar House. An annual event was the Charles Morgan Cattle Show, and the usual course of Christmas parties, children's parties and the servants' ball. There was a Boxing Day hunt, and the whole season ended with the great 'Fancy Ball', a traditional Twelfth Night masquerade party held on the evening of the last day of Christmas, 5 January. A huge cake, called the Twelfth Cake, contained a bean, and whoever found the bean in their slice of cake became master of revels or 'king' for the evening. These parties at one time consisted of the guests being paired off by virtue of their costume characters – so Signor Baritonini would pair with Madame Trills, for example. Local stationers were

commissioned to provide the character cards which guests would be given at random. Some of these events are referred to in this report from the Shrewsbury Chronicle *of 22 January 1813.*

FESTIVITIES AT TREDEGAR According to an ancient custom, the mansion of Sir Charles Morgan Bart. was thrown open at Christmas, and the usual hospitality reigned till the tenth instant. Upwards of sixty persons of the first distinction had accommodation in the house; amongst whom we noticed Lord William Somerset, Sir Isaac Coffin-Greenly, Sir Mark and Miss Wood, Sir Robert and Misses Salisbury, Colonel, Mrs and the Misses Molyneux, Mr, Mrs and the Misses Jones, Mr Edwin, Mrs Wyndham, Mr and Mrs Grant and family, Mr and Misses Benyon, Masters Lewis, Lascelles, Macnamaras, Tyler, Knight etc. etc.; and it being the rule of the house never to suffer either the servants or guests to depart for as long as . . . can be found they also were entertained.

On Twelfth Night a disappointment occurred, the masks and dresses not arriving in time, which seemed to dispirit all except the worthy Baronet, to whom it afforded much satisfaction, as it gave him an opportunity of soliciting the neighbours to assemble the day following – this was readily acceded to and on the 7th instant perhaps a better masquerade was never witnessed.

At two o'clock supper was announced, when a greater display of beauty in fancy dresses of unrivalled taste and elegance never appeared; and the profusion of diamonds and pearls added much to the splendour of the scene. Soon after supper the merry dance commenced, and was kept up with spirit until a late hour.

Three days in the week were devoted to the Chase, and the intervening days to Shooting, and to Horse and Foot Races; in short, Tredegar was one continued scene of mirth, good humour and jocularity. Champaign, Burgundy, white and red

Guests dressed for the famous Tredegar House 'Fancy Party', the
Twelfth Night Ball, *c.* 1910.

Hermitage, and every expensive wine was served with the utmost profusion during the whole festivities.

The music was excellent. Sir Charles Morgan's band ushered the company through the great hall to the dining parlour, where three sets of musicians alternatively played during dinner.

Upwards of one hundred servants dined every day, who were regaled with the best cheer, and abundance of Welsh

Christmas house guests getting ready for a morning ride at Tredegar House, 1920s.

Ale. Amidst all this gaiety, Sir Charles was not unmindful of the sufferings of the indigent; he most liberally caused new clothing to be provided and distributed amongst the poor of the neighbouring parishes.

The Masquerade Ball – or 'Fancy Ball' as the House traditionally called it – for Christmas 1812 had over sixty guests, and the costume list gives an excellent picture of how the guests appeared. It is interesting that from a world of wonderful costumes at their disposal, many of these society guests chose peasant costumes or costumes from the 'lower orders'! Some of the spaces are still blank, as the list was obviously written before all the information had been finalized.

Mrs Molyneaux – Domino
Miss Molyneaux – Quaker
Miss M. Molyneaux – Country girl
Miss Harriet Molyneaux – Beggar
Mrs Grant – Domino
Miss Grant – French ?
Miss Letitia Grant – Nun
Miss ? – Mendicant
Mrs Hale – Deaf and dumb woman
Miss Parkin – Nun
Mrs Dene – Sybil
Miss Dene – Beggar woman
Miss Bunyan – Fish woman
Miss Bunyan – Ballad singer
Mrs Edwin – ?
Mrs Wyndham – Fortune teller
Mrs Jones – ?
Miss Jones – ?
Miss Elvira Jones – ?
Mrs Jones – Old woman
Miss Grant – Gypsy
Mrs Leyson – Old woman
Miss Leyson – Old spinster
Miss Caroline Leyson – ?
Miss Wood – Gypsy
Miss Salisbury – House girl
Miss Elizabeth Salisbury – ?
Mrs Jones & Miss Lewis –
    Sultana and black boy
Miss Morgan – Witch
Miss G. Morgan – Beggar woman
Miss Morgan – Boy
Mr Henry Grant – Jew
Mr Hale – Major sturgeon

Lord William Somerset –
    Hair dresser
Sir Issac Greenly – Ghost
Sir Nathan Wood? –
    Recruiting sergeant
Col. Molyneux – Carter
Mr Francis Lewis – Pilgrim
Capt. Taylor – Doctor
Mr Knight – Cobbler
Mr Jones – Watchman
Mr ? – Beggar man
Mr John Leyson – Sailor
Mr Richardson – Devil
Mr Bannermann – Knave
    of Hearts
Mr J. Bannermann –
    Cardinal
Mr Salisbury – Countryman
Mr Charles Salisbury –
    Ballad singer
Mr Henry Salisbury –
    Orange woman
Mr Robert Salisbury – Punch
Mr Lascelles – Gretna Green
    Parson
Dr Mace? – Countryman
Sir Charles Morgan –
    Housemaid
Mr Morgan – Blue devil
Mr George Morgan – Orange
    Jew boy
Mr Augustus Morgan –
    Orange girl

The lists of the parties throughout the 1830s and '40s included much more imaginative characters, such as Mary Queen of Scots, Henry the Eighth and Puritan lady in 1832, a Mistress of the Moon, Oodle and Doodle and Sir Thomas Morgan (1668) from 1834, while later parties had Tyrolean peasant, Old English barons, Greeks and Butterflies. The servants' parties were by all accounts every bit as extravagant. Lord Tredegar made a traditional appearance at the top door, to descend the steps and begin the dancing. It was not uncommon for one of the family to loan a favoured personal servant an outfit for the evening, and one Daisy Masters, now in her seventies, remembers her mother and father, who were both in service at the House in the early part of the twentieth century,

The Servants' Christmas Ball at Tredegar House, mid-nineteenth century. Note that the servants stayed in their uniforms, as they were still 'on call'.

*talking of the servants' balls. Her mother was loaned a blue
silk chiffon 'flapper' style dress with darker blue sequins and
stars on it. But no matter how late the party went on, the
servants still had to be up at the crack of dawn the next day to
grind the wheels of the great house, blackleading the grates and
laying the fires, preparing the meals, cleaning the floors and
dusting and polishing before the household awoke. We now
return to high society with this ditty written by one wag after
the 1812 party.*

Tredegar concluded with a grand Masquerade.
Some of the party in grief and deep sorrow
Ordered the chaises and off on the morrow.
Capt. Ellis and wife for Abergavenny
Having as gypsies told the fortunes of many.
Mr Price and his lady to Llanwern were to dine
Miss Davis obliged the party to join
Slaughters and Richardson went the next day
Hearts were so heavy not a word could they say.
Oh! had you but seen the Kirkbys in grief
And several young beaux offering relief
Miss Molyneux next alas! The poor creatures,
How cruelly grief distorted their features;
The decorous ladies before that they parted
Declared one and all they were quite broken hearted
Treharris and Miss Richards from Lochtraheen
So burdened with tears, not fit to be seen.

*Naturally such gatherings were well reported in the society
news of the day. The family archives include notes written in
longhand by reporters of the various local papers, such as this
one from 1835, entitled 'Tredegar Festivities,
Monmouthshire'.*

Dance programmes from the Tredegar House Servants' Ball.

The noble invasion of Sir Charles Morgan has been for the last fortnight a scene of the most brilliant hospitality. The party though not so numerous as on former occasions has had to boast of much beauty and fashion. The kind and unaffected attention of the worthy baronet and his amiable daughters rendered their festive greetings truly delightful.

On Monday last the annual masquerade took place and considering the smallness of the party went off with much mirth and merriment. The characters were few but well chosen. Amongst the most prominent we noticed the noble lord as an Old English baron, the Miss's Morgans as Quakers were both noted and much admired. Lord and Lady Wm

Somerset a Scotch baron and his wife, pictures of conjugal felicity. Lord Sinclair Beaufort as Honest Jack Tar, a character he has been supported with Genl Molyneux, Sir Lucius O'Trigger, Mr and Mrs Humphrey, admirably shaped in ancient costume . . .

. . . accompanied Miss Humphrey as Lady Snaresworth, in which characters they spared neither friends nor foes . . .

Mr J. Bannerman as young Wilding from Fosters farce of the year, boasting of favours from ladies he never received and assignations never made . . .

Capt. Ellis as a bear! . . . Mrs Botto and the Miss's Seymour [as] Spanish ladies formed a beautiful group. Mr Lascelles as Falstaff not only worthy himself, but the cause of mirth in others . . .

Col. Lewis and Mr Darby as men of fashion . . .

The Masque was much enlivened by a party of Troubadors who delighted the company by singing several charming Spanish and French airs. The rest of the company consisted of flower girls, country men and the usual melange on such occasions.

Supper took place at two o'clock and the tables were furnished with every delicacy the season affords.

The following report, entitled 'Tredegar Christmas Festivities'
was made sometime in the 1830s or '40s.

Tredegar, the seat of Sir Charles Morgan, Bart., has this winter been, as usual, a scene of festive gaiety. Those Christmas parties which have been continued without interruption for more than 25 years, have assumed a rather Patriarchal character, as the venerable baronet has this winter had the gratification of assembling round him every member of his family; all his sons and daughters, and his 24 grandchildren congregated at the same time beneath his venerable roof.

Unlike many modern parties, the guests were expected to make considerable efforts for the entertainment of others. Often these efforts would take the form of party games, charades being a particular favourite, although many of the games would be quite unfamiliar to the modern partygoer. Little ditties or poems were often composed, sometimes passing comment upon, or poking gentle fun at, other guests. These poems would be read out to the assembled guests. No doubt a forfeit would have to be paid by an intended victim who roundly protested his innocence despite all evidence to the contrary. Below are two examples in the same handwriting found in the Tredegar Archives, probably written in the early 1820s.

MR G. ROUS ON BEING SEVERELY SMITTEN BY MISS S. BUSHEY

Led by wanton idle play
Cupid spied the other day
And seeing that my heart was free
From love's omnipotent decree
He made a deep incision there
To see what more than common air
Had kept me from his quiver free
And darts so often aim'd at me
He enter'd – but too soon the wound
Not long divisible – your sound
And left within the rosy God
Who erring where he ne'er had trod
Now rudely winds my heart about
Trying to find a passage out.

Miss Jane Homfray
To Tredegar did come free
But alas! it too true is
She went bound to Lewis.

*Christmas time at Tredegar was very important for the local
tradesmen in Bristol and in Newport. About a dozen firms
were dependent on the patronage of the house in Bristol alone,
and a further six or seven in Newport. The grocery bill in the
early 1830s seems to have been twice as much as the wages bill
for the whole household. The seasonal house party in 1838
accounted for the slaughter of 5 bullocks, 29 sheep, 10 pigs,
1 lamb and 2 calves. Tredegar's meat-storing rooms in the
cellars of the older part of the house are still painted blue to
discourage flies, and the huge meat hooks still hang from the
ceilings. Candles were a huge expense, especially to keep
Christmas bright during the six-week season: in 1818 the
December/January bill was for 1,153 candles.*

from

A Monmouth Mummers' Play

*The traditional mummers' play is the same basic tale of the
good St George beating the pagan knight, who is then brought
back to life by the appearance of the quack doctor and his
miraculous pills. Each region has its own local variations, often
of a topical nature, and characters. Sometimes similarities
appear in regions far apart, as travelling players took their*

*play from one part to another. The following undated play,
which was found in a Monmouth bookshop, was reputedly put
on at the Punchbowl Inn on Agincourt Square, where they used
to serve hot punch, the players on a fine Christmas spilling out
on to the square with their plays.*

Here comes I old Father Christmas, welcome or welcome not
I hope old Father Christmas will never be forgot.
But old Father Christmas he has but short time to stay,
I be come to show you pleasure to while the time away.

I travel far I travel near
I come now for a jar o' your Christmas beer –
If it be your best
Then in heaven I pray your soul to rest,
If your ale it be small
We show you no cheer at all.

Walk in, Room, again I say,
And pray good people clear the way
Walk in Room.

Enter Room
God bless you all ladies and gentlemen,
Its Christmastime and I come again
My name is Room, one sincere and true,
A merry Christmas I wish to you.
A King of Egypt is for to display
A noble champion without delay.
A noble doctor too I declare
And his bag of tricks bring up the rear.
And let the Egyptian King straightway appear!

Enter Egyptian King
Here come I the Egyptian King

38

Above: mummers, *c.* 1780. Below: mummers, new style – collecting for charity in Monmouth, 1980.

Whose mighty deeds round the globe doth ring
No other champion but me excels
Except my son-in-law St George.
Indeed that wondrous knight whom I so dearly love
Whose mortal deeds the world so well approve
The hero whom no dragon could affright,
Come, valiant champion bold, your warlike ardour to display
And show good England's enemies dismay.
Walk in St George!

Enter St George
Here come I St George,
That valiant champion bold,
And with my sword and spear,
I've won three crowns of gold.
I slew the Dragon 'He'
And brought him to the slaughter
By which I gained fair Sabra
The King of Egypt's daughter . . .

Enter the Turkish Knight
Here come I the Turkish Knight
Come from the Turkish land to fight
I'll fight St George that man of valour bold
And if your blood is hot
I soon will make it cold.

St George draws his sword
Large words my worthy friend
I am the man for thee
Therefore prepare yourself to fight with me
Or else I'll slay thee instantly!

They fight, the Turkish knight falls, then rising to one knee says
Oh pardon me St George,

Oh pardon me I crave
Oh give me but my life
And I will be thy slave!

St George immediately regrets killing the knight, and calls for a doctor
Is there no doctor to be found to cure a deep and deadly wound?

Enter Doctor with large bag which he opens
I can cure lovesick maidens, jealous husbands, squalling wives and brandywine doused dames
With one touch of my tripple liquid or a touch of Jerusalem balm.
And here is a pill called Pompomlouf
Guaranteed to bring man back to life.

> *He stoops and puts a pill on the knight's tongue. The knight jumps up, fully convinced of the error of his evil ways, and becomes a Christian and faithful servant of St George. Local people differ in their stories of the play. Some say that Father Christmas had a wife whom he accidentally kills, and the doctor is again called in. Other versions say that Robin Hood, Maid Marian and Little John are brought in. This latter seems to fit in with the Chepstow play (see next section).*

from

The Chepstow Christmas Play

*Further down the River Wye is Chepstow, which in the early
1800s was twice the population of nearby Cardiff. Their
nineteenth-century Christmas mummers' play varied slightly
from the Monmouth version, as this extract shows.*

Enter Father Christmas
In comes I Old Father Christmas
Christmastide or Christmas not
I hope Father Christmas will neer be forgot.
A mug of your strong beer, to make us dance and sing,
And the money in our pockets is a very fine thing.
Christmas comes but once a year
And when it comes it brings good cheer.
Roast Beef and Brawn and swete Mince pie
No one love it better than I.

*Other characters in this version include jolly old man or
woman, a soldier and Little John.*

A Borders Farmhouse Christmas Before 1914

ANON

This account was sent in after a radio request for memories from Wales and the Borders which we made in 1981. It had an Abergavenny postmark, but was otherwise anonymous. Still, we can assume from the postmark that the farm was in the rural borders of ·Monmouthshire, and from the account and names used, most probably from the northern extremity of Monmouthshire, probably around Grosmont or Skenfrith. Abergavenny could easily have been the nearest market town. The farm was obviously a very wealthy one, and may have been a defunct manor, still with its farmlands around rented out to tenant farmers.

Christmas was a happy occasion, but only twenty-four hours, not a week or more of parties as in modern times. Parents kept many little secrets, and I am sure it added to the importance of the day – anticipation and hope filled one for

weeks, plus the anxiety of making or buying in total secrecy the things one was giving the parents.

Holly was cut beforehand from trees on our farm, and stored in a cold outhouse. Many paperchains were made in the evenings in the kitchen. Mistletoe was brought home one week in advance from the market town, as were the cut flowers; with careful choice and management – only coal fires and no tobacco smoke – these lasted three to four weeks. In evenings when the rooms were very warm, the flowers were moved to the hall table, a much fresher place, with tiled floor, stairwell unheated and many doors frequently opened.

Most households had maids, and in addition to our three there was a gardener-handyman and a strong lad, fifteen or sixteen, who lived in. Evidently our household ways met with their approval, and one Christmas a maid asked if her sister might come to share food and fun, being willing to help a little in return! No wages asked, she just wanted to join in. Of course she was allowed to come, and when we had a vacancy she came to help us permanently. Each man employed on the farm was given a joint of meat in proportion to the size of his family, and asked beforehand whether he wanted beef or pork.

Christmas Eve was a great day – while decorations were put up indoors, my parents drove with horse and trap, no matter how bad the weather, to fetch this meat order. They also brought oranges and boiled sweets, to give an orange and half a pound of sweets to every child of every employee. Outdoors, every possible preparation was done to reduce essential work on the 25th, to give our men as much free time as possible, yet care for the animals. With a hundred cows to be milked morning and afternoon by hand, and fed and cleaned out, everyone was obliged to work two and a half hours each at each end of the day, Christmas included.

When work ended on the 24th, each man came to the house to receive the meat, oranges and sweets, and a gold half-

sovereign for himself and his wife – quite a sum then. This really was the start of the excitement for me, quickly followed by hanging up the 'kissing bunch' – how could it have that name with no mistletoe in it? It was two wooden hoops, one forced inside the other, and their frames covered with ivy and tinsel and decorated with flags and a few baubles. Also hung high was a holly bunch, from which red apples hung on strings. A ham, an ox tongue and a turkey were cooked ready for Boxing Day. I never ate hot turkey until I was grown up, though ours were home-reared. Christmas dinner was traditionally sirloin roast beef and plum pudding, cheese and celery.

In the evening of the 24th, the 'Guisers' came, singing and miming – they were completely disguised, and rather frightening to me when they arrived at the back door and crowded into the kitchen. As soon as they were refreshed with mince pies and tea and departed, I was hurried to bed so that I could get up when the band came. Fires had been banked up, large copper kettles on the stove, meat dishes filled with mince pies and slices of fruit cake, and large trays laden with cups. Whether anyone stayed awake I never knew.

The band, which had played carols at houses all the two miles from the next village, always assembled silently on our front lawn just before midnight. As the church clock struck twelve they began to play 'Christians Awake' – everyone in the house rushed downstairs and the front door was propped open, our large well-lit hall sending a stream of light out to the garden, fairyland to me at such an hour. At four years old I was first rushed to a window to see and hear, and then downstairs (in a dressing-gown amongst strange men!) to eat cake and drink milk amid this jolly throng which trooped in for tea and food. This *was* Christmas to me. No one chided me to rush back to bed; only when the band went out to play at least two more pieces, and after much well-wishing, did we go upstairs.

Carollers calling at the big
houses: a nineteenth-century
engraving.

I must have slept well after this for Santa Claus never failed
to come, and on one occasion brought a large wooden doll's-
house without waking me.

The tree was set up and dressed after the children were in
bed, never earlier in the week. That was another magic
moment, coming down on Christmas morning to see a
dressed tree where there had been no sign of one the previous
evening. In our house, the door of that room must have been
locked before the arrival of the band. During the day gifts for
the indoor staff were placed around the tree, our house guests
(usually old friends from London) giving such acceptable
extras as a leather purse or prayer book. My mother knew that
the maids hoped for elegant lacy aprons with matching caps
far more expensive than those normally provided as part of
their uniform – she gave these, but added something personal
as well. Family gifts were on the breakfast table.

Everyone went to church at 11 a.m. for a simple friendly service, the beef roasting meanwhile. In the afternoon anyone who wished took a walk, maids included, or even had a chance to look at one's presents again.

At 6.30 p.m. we all gathered in the front kitchen near the tree, and sat down together at one table for a high tea – cold meats, Christmas cake and mince pies, plus crackers. This meal included a huge pork pie surrounded by sparklers, a sight which thrilled me and I have never seen it elsewhere. My mother had bought them when available at Guy Fawke's Day, and stored them in a tin.

After tea, one of our friends would hand out the gift parcels, and there would be talk and perhaps simple games for about an hour. The holly bunch being much too high for me, my close friend the gardener could be relied on to lift me up to get at least one apple, my mother scolding him, amid laughter, for such favouritism – one was expected to jump up to such a height! It was understood that fun could continue as long as they wished, also food and tea, on condition that the gardener helped with the washing up, as all had to be up at the same early hour next morning.

Christmas was over when we returned to the sitting room, probably around 8.30 p.m. – I was sent to bed and the grown-ups could relax – no parties, no drinking, a simple happy time together.

On Boxing Day men friends came early to rough shooting. Lunch was carried out to them, using for coffee the one-gallon jugs used for tea during haymaking. Dinner was at 5 p.m., the cold turkey etc. sometimes augmented with a couple of hot roast ducks, and followed by trifle and jellies. The farm resumed its normal routine, except for one man who handled the ferrets, gutted rabbits and cleaned our gun if it had been used. My father didn't shoot, and most men preferred to use their own.

Boro Divvus

MONMOUTHSHIRE GYPSIES

*During the first half of the twentieth century, gypsies were a
common sight as they travelled throughout Monmouthshire and
the neighbouring counties of Hereford and Gloucestershire. They
worked in the fields, hop-picking, apple- and pear-picking,
and, around Christmas, carol-singing. Here are a few memories
gleaned from a wonderful 87-year-old man called Ned, who
was born on the road in a traditional vardo and still lives on
the road with his dog.*

We used to call Christmas the Great Day, 'Boro Divvus' my
grandad used t' say it were. We had a great fire all through the
day med wi' Ashwood. We do it because, so story goes, Our
Saviour were born on the Great Day in a field like us, an' he were
brought up by the camp fire med of ash like us, an' because the
ash giv' away the hiding place of Our Saviour, so we allus med a
great ashwood fire. The pines an' suchlike kept quiet an' so kept
their leaves all winter, but the ash told, and lost its winter cover
as a punishment, an' that's why we burn 'er on the Great Day.

The women do most o' the rituals, not so many now, but
me granny used t' collect bits o' wood, twigs an' suchlike, an'
put them outside the vans. In the evenin' each family would
put straw on t' floor, an fruit and nuts from t' woods on t'
table, but no meats of any kind, an' then the menfolk went
out to find somethin' – nothing valuable you understand, just
a twig or two, that sort o' thing. Then they threw all twigs

an' wood on t' ground an' burned it, sayin' 'No one know we'm bin out a-stealin' this night.' This were a charm to mek sure they would find things easy all the year. That were allus on Chrismus Even. On the Great Day, my fether did do somethin' wi' water and wood and coins, enterin' the van he'd say 'May we 'ave sweet water to drink, and enough coin to manage.' An' the wood were thrown on t' fire, an' if it sparked well that were a sign that the livestock would thrive well.

Another account from a Romany who now lives on a council estate and keeps her name quiet so that neighbours will not identify her.

A great effort was put into the Christmas meal, with cutlery and china laid out properly where space allowed. There was usually a goose which had spent the year guarding the campsites and foraging in the hedgerows, and from September on would be fed extra with corn made into a mash with leftovers. Mam would stuff ours with a concoction of mashed potatoes, the gooseliver, dried wild mushrooms, eggs and roasted apples, and any herbs such as she could get, thyme, sage, parsley, balm and a few juniper berries. We would eat it with turnips and baked potatoes and apple sauce, and our winecup was usually homemade, like elderberry, or maybe cider or perry.

There were lots of customs borrowed from the 'Gorgios' [non-gypsies], especially the begging customs. The women went out on St Thomas's Day. If they went round the farms they got a measure of corn in some areas, and breadcakes in others. The kids went out at New Year down your way [south of Monmouth down to Chepstow areas] 'monty-ing'. They would stick an apple with twigs and a few nuts and berries, and go round to the houses singing. It was supposed to be bad luck not to accept the apple offering, and give a few coins or sweets or something else in return.

The menfolk often joined in the farming customs, as they were helping the farmers. One custom my father did was 'burning the bush'. All the men would carry a bush made of tied twigs all around the fields to drive out evil spirits. The last bush to be burned was then saved, as a charm, until the next year. I've still got the last one my father had; it was given to him, together with a jug of cider, for his payment.

They also went and sang to the fields and the animals — this was done with lots of cider and perry — but had all but gone by the time my father was born just before the Great War. The usual payment was a stone jug of ale, cider or pear perry, and if they were lucky, a shilling in their pockets and maybe even a plumcake, if the farmer's wife was generous. There was one who would make three dozen plumcakes to give to all the farmhands and helpers at the Wassail, as it was called.

And of course they would all go a-carolling, women and children. Singing comes easy to our people. In the days before

Harriet Jones, the gypsy carol singer well known around Monmouthshire and Herefordshire in the late nineteenth–early twentieth century.

televisions, after dinner everyone would get together around a big fire, tell stories and have a singsong. I only know what my mam told me really. There was one old woman [Harriet Jones] my grandmother used to speak of who was quite well known all around for her carols. She was lettered, and could read the songs off the old broadsheets, so she had her own songs, like 'Christ Made a Trance', as well as the printed ones like 'Remember Man'. She had a fine voice, deep they say it was, like a man's, but sweet and pure like an angel! Well that's what I heard anyway.

One custom at Christmas was called 'deceiving the Gorgio'. Someone had to leave camp, and later that evening come a-calling like a stranger. It was always a man. The women would invite him to sit by the fire and have some refreshment, and bring a cushion. But every time the 'visitor' went to sit, they would pull the cushion away, whispering, 'As I deceive you so may I deceive the Gorgio'. After three tries, the visitor was allowed to sit and eat, and was traditionally offered sugar, water, black coffee and a special flat cake.

Gypsy Carollers

The carollers seem to have been very active around the eastern area of Monmouthshire, especially where the county bordered Herefordshire and Gloucestershire. A number of broadsheets, that is carols printed on a single sheet for street singers, were published in Birmingham and distributed down as far as Monmouth; many of the old folk of Monmouthshire remember

*the gypsy singers before the Second World War. The following
extract is from Mary Ellen Leathers's* Folklore of
Herefordshire *(1912), taken from notes made by Ralph
Vaughan Williams; its accounts coincide with the
Monmouthshire memories. The 'Mrs Whatton' may well be the
old woman with the angel's voice recalled in the extract above.*

Mrs Whatton repeated this carol to me in a gypsy van; her
daughter sang it into the phonograph. All the gypsies who
have sung for me know the carol, and the usual version had
'Sunday view' in the first line; none could explain what the
first verse meant. I think the version with a similar tune
noted by Miss Burne (*Shropshire Folklore*, 1910) must be from
the same family of gypsies. The first line is probably a
corruption of something quite different, or it may be a
fragment of a legend of the Creation now forgotten.

> Christ made a trance one Sunday at noon
> He made it with his hand
> And made the sun clear all off the moon
> Like the waters on dry land.

*Carols were generally songs sung at any time of year, especially
by the gypsies in the area. It was the custom to have a verse or
two relating to a specific feast, such as Christmas, so that the
carols could be sung with equal aplomb at all such traditional
times! The following carol, 'Divrus {Dives} and Lazarus',
printed in a broadsheet, was found in the Robin Hood Inn in
Monmouth and given to us in the 1960s.*

> As it fell out on a light dully day,
> When Divrus made a feast
> And he invited all his friends
> grand gentry of the best.

As with all medieval carols and ballads, this one tells (in fifteen verses) of the life and death of Divrus. The last verse for the Christmas singing is as follows.

At merry Christmas time
And among good Christians all
This Christmas car-i-ol might be sung
In either house or hall.

Abergavenny's Magi

FRED HANDO

During the English Reformation of the sixteenth–seventeenth centuries, many private homes of 'recusants' (people who observed the Roman Catholic faith) had secret rooms where visiting priests could celebrate mass. This was a dangerous activity, because if caught the punishment was often hanging, drawing and quartering. To be bold enough actually to have a shrine or altar which could be identified by the authorities was asking for trouble. However, just such a find was made in Abergavenny, and with a Christmas emphasis. This story comes from Fred Hando, who was for many years a correspondent for the South Wales Argus, *and a fount of all knowledge on the lore and history of his beloved Monmouthshire (printed in the* Argus, 15 January 1954).

In 1907, when workmen removed the partition in the top story of an ancient house in Cross Street, Abergavenny, they discovered a secret chamber, twenty-three feet by ten.

On the sloping ceiling at the east end were the remains of a remarkable mural painting, four feet two by two feet nine inches, representing the *Adoration of the Magi*. The workmen had come across a treasure which had been hidden for two and a half centuries. The fresco with its underlying plaster was carefully removed, placed under glass in an oak frame and taken into 'private custody'. Thus the loveliest mural painting in Gwent was once again lost to view, and enquiries were fruitless.

Then Mrs Barber, wife of my friend 'Ali', while buying sweets in a shop in Cross Street heard the shopkeeper saying that she had discovered a big mural painting behind a dresser in one of her rooms. When 'Ali' and I saw it, we recognized it

The *Adoration of the Magi*: Fred Hando's sketch of the Abergavenny painting as it was in 1954.

at once as the lost *Adoration*. It is truly, in spite of much flaking in the lower half, a masterpiece. Mrs Francis (aged eighty-one) who was and still is living in the house, told me that when it was discovered in 1907 a certain museum offered £800 for it. Discerning Monmouthshire folk will see at once that its value is beyond rubies.

Under the black roof of the penthouse on the right is the ox rendered with the poise and forthright technique of a pre-historic cave painting. Dressed in deep blue the Virgin Mary, with a circlet halo above her head, nurses the Holy Child, whose halo is more ornate. The star in the East directs its rays toward the Child. On the left is a Wise Man with an hypnotic eye . . . Where are the other Magi? Maybe their kneeling figures occupied the lost foreground but there is nothing left which would help us to decide, and the vacant space on the Virgin's dress is not wide enough to hold a standing figure . . .

This then was the altarpiece in the secret Catholic chapel in the house of Thomas Gunter, the seventeenth-century Abergavenny attorney. My sketch shows the painting [as it was in 1954] but one of the Wise Men is missing, and it seemed to me that we should never know where the others were portrayed.

Fred Hando was like a terrier when presented with a local mystery: he delved and poked until he tracked it down. Here, in another entry from the South Wales Argus, *(22 January 1954), we read how he solved the mystery.*

Mr John Collett, our borough librarian, set his staff to search among his archives. One of his bright young ladies unearthed in the 'Haines Collection' a photograph taken of the painting before its removal, and on that print . . . we were able to see clearly behind the figure remaining, the other two Magi, one bearing a gift . . .

Mr Hando then describes at great and fascinating length how he proceeded to solve the mystery of the secret room – how it had been hidden in an attic, without any stairwell, for 250 years – and of the recusant priests and martyrs who worshipped there. His delving did eventually turn up the missing Magi when, some months later, a Mrs Parry, who lived in the central part of the divided house, contacted him with the news that she had discovered a small frame with the two remaining Magi. But he does not say what happened to the painting, and again this seemed to be lost. Then, in 1982, Christmas Archives International set up an exhibition of Christmas through the ages, in the recently re-opened museum in Abergavenny Castle. There, over the fireplace, was the missing painting, fully restored with the two parts joined; it had been donated in July 1961. An entry from the souvenir museum guide states that 'it is thought to have been the reredos to an altar in a secret chapel, and was probably painted by the priest himself in the guise of a travelling house painter or builder'. It remains in the museum still.

An Exhibition of Christmas Past

In 1982 Abergavenny received international acclaim with its first Christmas Exhibition at the Castle Museum. The event was filmed by NBC Coast to Coast American television, and well covered by several local newspapers and television.

As the brochure described: 'The intimate surroundings of Abergavenny Castle Museum lend themselves delightfully to the exhibition of Christmas Past. Here, in what can be termed as a 'cosy' atmosphere, one can imagine the more easily, the thoughts and feelings and atmosphere of those long ago Christmases represented by the items on display. We bring you essentially the Christmas of Dickens, but with glimpses of other times from Roman right down to the 1950s, and we hope you will take away with you some of the Spirit of Christmases Past to enrich your own Christmases present.'

Items on display ranged from Christmas cards, Christmas trees in little 'room' settings – one with Santa Claus and lots of toys the other a more sedate affair with a round trimmed box tree decorated with ribbons and attended by two ladies in Georgian dress – Christmas decorations and evergreens, including a fifteenth-century Holy Bough, with whittled figures of the Holy Family nestling inside a decorated and be-ribboned double hoop of evergreens. Everything, in fact, from the first electric tree lights, to pantomime posters, Christmas jewellery, crackers, cakes and books.

The exhibition also held demonstrations in Christmas floral arrangements, given by the museum curator, Mrs Anna Tucker, and Mrs Lorraine O'Shea, one of the exhibition assistants. So many people turned up for the exhibition and the demonstrations that at times it got quite crowded.

Downstairs in the old castle kitchen, which was well garlanded in traditional style, was a Mari Lwyd (see 'The Mari Lwyd' extract above). Its grinning horse's skull was decked with colourful ribbons and hung with a white sheet, under which the man who would have operated the Mari Lwyd would have stood. On the table was a Christmas cake decorated with orange peel and described by a lady who lived deep in the Monmouthshire countryside, just on the borders

with Wales proper: 'We kept both turkeys and geese to fatten up for Christmas market, but we never had them ourselves, they were too expensive and only for market. We used to have a fattened cockerel, and a bit of ham. Our cake wasn't decorated with icing. Mam used to candy the peel from an orange or two, and make a syrup with the juice. On to the fruit cake she would pour the syrup, and then the curls of candied peel, and that was our Christmas cake. Other people did that too in our area, I remember.'

The museum benefited from gifts of cards and other Christmas donations by the folk of Abergavenny, showing what a very Christmassy people they were indeed!

'Monty'

ROSE JONES

Mrs Rose Jones, who is now in her eighties, still lives on the Trelleck Road in Tintern, which she made her home after marrying a local man during the Second World War. Here she describes the evolution of her adopted village and the changes in Christmas custom that accompanied the rapid increase in population since 1945.

We never had a large family Christmas. My family originated in the Scottish Highlands, so any aunts, uncles and cousins were a long way away. We only had two children of our own.

Children offering 'Monty' in the Chepstow area, early twentieth century.

When I married my husband during the war, he was the local builder. He employed a man from an old local Welsh family who had two sons. Every New Year's Day these two boys would call at the house with what they called a 'Monty', which was an apple standing on three twigs, with some other twigs and spices stuck into it. I would give the boys a sixpence or some such in return for this Monty. We would keep it for luck until it rotted away.

As the boys got bigger and the village changed, we never thought that this would end. You always knew these two boys would call. Of course one year they didn't, and it was some while before one realized that it was never going to happen again!

Carol singing was quite common as well. It was very safe for children. There was no 'Neighbourhood Watch' in those days; you didn't need it! Everyone knew everybody else, nobody locked their doors, and there were few cars about.

It all started to change during the war as the men were off fighting and most of the women worked in the armament factory outside Chepstow. Most mothers didn't have much time to prepare for Christmas. That meant there were few people in church: everyone was too busy with war work. The children didn't have much encouragement to go to church, what with their mothers working all the time. Churches were much more restricted in those days. I remember every seasonal feast had its colours. Easter was always yellow with some white, the flowers were always daffodils. Whitsun was white flowers with a touch of red, harvest was lovely because every colour was there, while Christmas was only green. Mistletoe was not allowed in the church, but there was plenty of ivy and holly with red berries. There wasn't the same glitz and glitter you see in churches nowadays.

A lot of the atmosphere went as we lost the local station, local rector, local school and village policeman. Since the war council houses were built outside the village, and people did

up the cottages as the prices went up. Some people started building houses in their gardens as new people moved in. When the Severn Bridge opened I was in favour of it as we could only get to England with the ferry, or round by Gloucester. We stopped being a backwater, but it became more like suburbia with new people who wanted all mod cons, and their gardens to look like suburban gardens. As that changed so did all the old feeling. Christmas changed too.

There wasn't much around, but the village was self-sufficient with two bakers and about four or five other shops including a butcher. Although there was a railway line from Tintern to both Monmouth and Chepstow, most things were produced locally.

Many of the cottages were quite dilapidated. I often wondered 'how come we are so healthy on so little?' Despite rationing you could always get enough butter and eggs. One baker kept chickens at Ferry Farm across the river: he would feed them on his leftover bread. We would always get a seven-pound chicken from him for Christmas, which we thought good enough. When turkeys became plentiful after the war, we never fancied them much.

I never had any particular recipes for Christmas, as I always cooked with a book in one hand: I still do! One never really notices the changes, they creep up on you. One day, there you are, no carol singers eating turkey, and you don't really remember exactly when things changed, you just suddenly find they have.

There was not a lot of Christmas shopping, as most people had to go by bus or train. We used to go to Newport or Gloucester by van for ours, so it wasn't so bad. Presents were straightforward after the war. We didn't have the choice of elaborate toys then. We always bought a Christmas tree from the forestry. I would decorate it at first, but my younger son used to help, then finally took over. The decorations were

nice, but not as fancy as nowadays. Few houses had electricity, so you wouldn't have lots of lights.

We always seemed to have someone ill at Christmas. One Boxing Day my son was taken into hospital in Newport. On another Boxing Day, 1946 I think it was, it started snowing, I was taken into a Newport hospital and stayed there for three weeks, so I didn't know how bad the snow was. It was a shock when I came out to see all the snowdrifts. The snow stayed until Easter!

One awful year all my Christmas memories were spoiled when my son was injured in a car accident on 4 January. He died soon afterwards. One has to come to terms with life as one gets older; Christmases aren't always happy.

Lost Ring – Christmas Queen

MEGAN JONES

Higher up the county in the industrial valleys above Abergavenny, the Twelfth Night cake custom survived into the twentieth century, with great yeast dough cakes being made for the whole family to gather round, a costly exercise at the best of times, and especially so for Megan Jones, who narrates this story.

It was only my second married Christmas, just after the end of the Great War it were, and me with a brand new babby. We all made our own cakes and suchlike in those days, mind it were a bit difficult just after the war to get all the ingredients, but everyone was that relieved they did the's best.

I were finding it difficult enough with the babby, without all the Christmas doings, but with my man working at the pit all hours t' keep us in the little 'ouse he'd got fer us, I 'ad to make do and not complain. I were luckier than most, a two-bedroom place all to us selves, my Jim got us – a nursery for all t' babbies, he said.

Anyway, there I was kneading me Christmas loaves, barm bracks really, made with yest and a bit of extra spice. One eye on the babby – even when 'e were asleep I felt I 'ad to watch 'im! An' by the time my man came in, there were six loaves all cooling. I felt so proud, and my Jim were never skimpy in 'is praise either. Then he said, 'Where's your ring, luv?' An' sure enough, when I looked, my finger were bare, with just the white mark where the ring 'ad been.

We looked *everywhere*. I were in tears, and Jim, thin-lipped tried to calm me. 'You'll upset t' babby if you go on like that girl,' he said. 'Bawling won't find it.' Well, we 'ad a fair miserable Christmas. My mam came for to stay for Christmas, being on her own like, and us 'aving all that lovely space. We were that proud being able to offer 'er a room all to 'erself! She was very upset about my ring. 'And you with a babby, Megan,' she said. 'How will people know you are wed?' Of course that sort of thing mattered in them days.

Jim's Mam and Da came on Twelfth Day. He managed to get both days off that year – so as we could 'ave a proper family do like the toffs did, 'e said, an' we was dead lucky, but it didn't help the festivities 'go with a swing' as they say – until tea-time. We 'ad just settled down to our Twelfth Day tea, Mam cut the last of my cakes, we'd always saved one big

one for Twelfth Day in our family, I can't say why, it's just a traditional thing to do like. Mam was saying what a nice texture it were, and out fell my ring! You could have knocked me down with a feather, honestly!

Everyone was that pleased, we all danced around the table, an' then Jim's Mam, who was older than anyone else there, Jim being youngest of twelve, remembered an old custom they 'ad in the big 'ouse where she was brought up, daughter of one of the undergardeners, she were. They 'ad a party for all the staff on the last day of Christmas and they 'ad this big cake with a bean baked in it, an' whoever got the bit with the bean was crowned king or queen of the party. So, because my ring was found in my Christmas loaf, Jim's Da made me a crown out of newspaper, and I was made the queen. I must 'ave looked real stupid prancing around with the local paper on my head, but we did enjoy the rest of our Christmas I can tell you!

The Grand Christmas Stock Show

No account of Monmouthshire Christmas would be complete
without the mention of the fat stock shows which were and still

*are part of every town, small and large, within the county. It
has been a major part of many a Monmouthshire man's or
woman's Christmas, either fattening stock for the best sale of the
year, bringing revenue to last many months, or buying in for the
landowners of the Big House, the Christmas retail trade or even
just a bird for the family table. The newspapers over the past
two centuries have devoted a major portion of their front pages
to detailed reports of these shows in Monmouth, Newport,
Chepstow, Usk, Abergavenny and other areas. Here are some
entries from the* Monmouthshire Beacon *over the centuries.*

19 December 1840 – SIR CHAS MORGAN'S ANNUAL CATTLE
SHOW This far-famed annual Christmas cattle show was held
at Court-y-Bella, the farm of Sir Charles Morgan, on
Wednesday last. The show was not so good as on former years,
but nevertheless it was as fine as could reasonably have been
expected, considering the prevalent sickness in cattle.

We experienced great difficulty in getting admittance to
the exhibition in the morning but this we apprehend was
owing to the want of proper instructions to the subs, who, in
hob-nail shoes, kicked at the privileges of the press. By the by,
we might not have been known as press-men at all . . .

The show of horses was very indifferent, but that of fat
stock was very fair in quantity and quality. The sheep were
above the average exhibition. Throughout the day the farm
was crowded with visitors, and we noticed Sir Charles
Morgan progressing from pen to pen, looking cheerful and
happy – long may he live to enjoy the fruits of his active
benevolence!

The dinner was held at the King's Head, Newport, at three
o'clock. Immediately after the removal of the cloths, Sir Chas
Morgan rose and said that since the establishment of the
Society in 1819, the sum of £3,300 had been expended in
cups (great cheering).

24 December 1859 – The butchers are arranging their hooks for a very good display of meat, and the Show this (Friday) night will bear comparison with any in former years . . .

22 December 1860 – THE GREAT CHRISTMAS CATTLE MARKET The grand market day that provides the most important item in our Christmas Fare – the Roast Beef of Old England – may be taken as the closing point of the fat stock year. From this point the grower of beef and mutton looks back upon his labours, proves his anticipatory estimates by actual results, and weighing cost against cattle, or rather, against what they have fetched, how far in rearing the fat ox for the consumer he has succeeded . . .

Post-war rationing took its toll, as we see from the report for
31 December 1950.

XMAS POULTRY MARKET Change from former days: the Monmouth Christmas Produce Market fixed by the Monmouth town council for Friday December 21st. One could imagine the array of dressed geese and chickens, of immense turkeys, and all the dealing and bartering which go to make up the market. These things were absent!!

A wander round the place showed a few dressed poultry being brought to a dealer but the bottom of the market where the poultry used to be sold was not in use.

Would you believe it? The chief feature of this market appeared to be a toy stall, fancy goods stall, rabbits and holly. The latter was the only display which gave the place a festive appearance. Then one examined the holly more closely. Most of it was in the shape of holly wreaths for graves! That springy Christmas feeling went!

However, once rationing was over, the stock markets were back
in business. In 1959 Rennie, Taylor and Till, the main

A Monmouthshire Christmas

Monmouthshire auctioneers, were advertising their 'Christmas fat stock show and sale' in Monmouth.

This show will be held only if the foot and mouth disease restrictions are withdrawn from the borough of Monmouth, on Saturday December 19th 1959. Prizes totalling £70 for six classes for cattle, two classes for sheep, three classes for pigs will be offered by the auctioneers and tradespeople together with the Monmouth Corporation Cup for the best fat beast.

One old farmer ('just say it's Bill, everyone knows me'), now in his late eighties and living in Birmingham, remembers a Chepstow ('or mebbe it were Newport') market sometime before the Second World War.

In them days we worked hard you know. I worked on our small farm which I shared, and I also had a job as a builder. We fattened up turkeys for Christmas, and a couple of pigs; we didn't have cows, and lamb wasn't so popular at Christmas, we got more for 'em at Easter, see.

Anyhow, we had this turkey-gobbler from a chick, the little 'uns brought it up, and although they was told that it were to be our Christmas dinner, they named it Fred and treated it like a pet. Christmas week came and Fred had been well fattened with corn, payed for outta me own pocket it were too. But Fred was still a'gobbling his welcome down the path everytime I came home from work! In the end, morning of Christmas Eve, I said to the wife, 'You'll have to get on and kill Fred else we'll have no Christmas dinner.'

'I'll do it today,' she promised me, and there was Fred that night, three o'clock of a Christmas Eve, coming down the path to greet me. They couldn't do it you see, so I was stamping mad, and went out wi' the axe. Ma shut all the curtains, an' I could hear the littl'uns howling like, and Ma

shouting, 'Shut it, or there'll be only boiling fowl and a bit of bacon for Christmas dinner.'

I took Fred into the barn, but I could not bring meself to do him in. He were one of the family, an' he looked at me with his beady eye as if to say, 'You wouldn't do that now would you?'

I went inside for me coat. They'd all gone into front of the house, so I just shouted, 'I'm off down to the poultry market,' an' by 'eck did I run! I were just in time to buy a couple of fat hens, an' that were our Christmas dinner!

No one nivver said a word about Fred. When I got back it were dark already, an' there were Fred, waiting by the gate – 'e nivver went in til mester came home, you see – that's loyalty for you. Well I couldn't 'ave killed him, could I?

We enjoyed us chickens, and wife had a bit of bacon boiled with spice and treacle, and we had turnips and roasted parsnips and potatoes. I nivver liked turkey meat anyway, too rich.

Monmouthshire's Ghosts – the Nuns of Usk Priory

No Christmas is complete without its complement of ghost stories, and Monmouthshire has its fair share. Never one to take such stories too seriously, I still cannot quite believe what happened to me on my first visit to Monmouthshire in December 1970.

One bright winter's day, shortly before Christmas, I went to Usk Priory. The property, a twelfth-century foundation, had in post-Reformation times become a gentleman's residence. After a fire, it was put on the market, and that is how I found it. Looking for something unusual to turn into a restaurant and hotel, here I had it all: even the adjoining churchyard was a place of pilgrimage – 'Goody, pilgrimage teas,' I thought. I had decided that I would buy the place even before I looked around. There were some builders working on a large house nearby, and I stopped to ask them the way into the grounds.

'You going in there alone?' asked one. I thought he was afraid for my dainty ankle on the upper floors, damaged by the fire! 'Of course,' I answered. 'I hope to buy it.'

'Needs a bit of doin' to it,' answered my companion doubtfully, who had indeed become so, escorting me through the grounds and to the house door. 'Are you sure you'll be

Usk Priory, December 1970. The photograph was taken on the same day as the events described in the story.

alright?' He seemed anxious not to come into the house, but said that if I did not return in half an hour, he would come and check on me.

'Leave it an hour, I want to get the feel of the place and take some measurements,' I rejoined. 'Don't worry, I'll scream if I fall through the floor.' I grinned at him as I turned the huge iron key in the lock.

I could not decide whether he was after a building job, or whether he had taken a shine to me in my Christmassy red hooded top – and a nose to match, no doubt. Anyway, I began my tour of the house. Five enormous rooms downstairs, a kitchen with a door leading out to the courtyard where I planned to have my pilgrimage teas. Along a corridor, which was obviously part of the old monastic cloister to a wonderful library, it turned the corner to a dead end, with signs of what was once an arched stone doorway, where the cloister would have carried on to meet the side door of the church, which still served as Usk parish church. I spent some time in the library, a big sunny room with huge Elizabethan windows. It

felt wonderfully welcoming, even in its poor state. After sandwiches and hot chocolate from a flask, I went upstairs.

The rooms here were just as impressive. The bathroom left a lot to be desired: just big enough for a bath and toilet, it was within the thickness of the wall over the cloister. There was also a narrow staircase leading up to the attics. Three times I started to climb that stairway, and yet could not continue. I was gripped with a fear which I could not explain. I am not a claustrophobic person – I hid in cupboards and holes as a child, and still like cosy poky corners. The room at the end of the house, over the library, was boarded off because this was where the fire had been. It had been the nuns' private chapel in the original convent, but subsequently, I assume, just another bedroom. There were no details about it on the estate agent's sheet.

I went back to the first room, and stood looking down on the courtyard, planning my restaurant, wondering if the church bells would edify or annoy hotel guests, and toying with the idea of asking my building acquaintance to come and give me an idea of costs to get things started. Then to my annoyance, in the dusk, I saw five nuns walking from the far end of the house, by the library, towards the church. 'Blow it!' I thought. 'Obviously someone else is after the place too.' The estate agent had said something about another interested party, but had I known nuns were after it, I would not have bothered getting all steamed up about the place. It was a perfect convent setting in the twelfth century, and still was in 1970, and I was not one to oust a convent of nuns just to have a restaurant!

When I left, the nuns were not in sight – probably looking around the church, I thought. Going round by the builder, who was packing up as I passed, I called to him that I was OK, and took the key back to the agents. They had already closed, as it was just after 6 p.m. so I put the keys through the

letterbox and went into the old pub on the square in front of the priory walls. Curiously the locals began asking questions, the whys, whos and wherefores of my visit. Somehow they already knew I had been up at the priory.

'You'll get plenty of help locally,' commented one. 'We're all keen to see the old place come to life agin.'

I said that I was very keen but would not make a decision unless the nuns who were there did not buy. There was a strange silence and a few guarded glances. Then someone said, in a quiet but confident, blustery way, 'Oh they old biddies won't buy, they bin there long enough already!'

As it happened, dry rot, a shortage of cash for the basic repairs and a few rules about not being able to have paying guests without all sorts of health and safety certificates which Usk Priory would definitely not get, spoilt my plans.

In recent years, I have moved back into Monmouthshire, and begun looking into local history and lore. Apparently, the original convent at Usk was for five nuns of the Benedictine order. At the suppression of the monasteries the five nuns were pensioned off, having given their allegiance to the king, thereby saving their lives and the probable destruction of the priory. The arched doorway I saw by the library was indeed part of the cloister, and the walkway where I saw the nuns was the way to the church. At 6 p.m. on a winter's evening, they could have walked along there to attend Vespers.

Several people have written about the sightings of the nuns, always along that walkway, or on the upper landing going to the house chapel. But I swear that I knew nothing of the history of the priory, nor the stories of the ghostly nuns when I visited just before Christmas in 1970!

A Christmas Petition

ADAM OF USK

*Adam of Usk was a Welshman who became a priest of Usk.
His life spanned the fourteenth and fifteenth centuries, and he
travelled very widely for his time. He kept a chronicle of both
local and national events, from 1377 to at least 1421. The
following entry tells how he went to Rome for Christmas 1404,
to make a Christmas petition on behalf of the nuns at Usk
Priory, whose chaplain he was and who were in poverty.*

On Christmas Day I was present at the papal Mass and the
banquet thereafter, together with my fellow auditors and
officers. And, in the first Mass, at the right horn of the altar
was placed a sword adorned with gold bearing on its upright
point a cap with two labels like a bishop's mitre, for this
purpose: that the emperor, if present, holding the naked
sword, should himself read, as deacon, as having been
anointed, the [Christmas] Gospel which begins, 'There went
out a decree from Caesar', and should have the same sword
from the Pope himself. But owing to the absence of the
emperor, a cardinal deacon read the gospel, and the Pope
delivered the sword to the Count of Malepella as being the
most noble present. In the same Mass, double Gospel and
Epistle are read, in Latin by two Latins, and in Greek by two

Greeks, for their satisfaction, for they say they were driven out of the Church . . .

I, the writer of this history, delivered to the Pope the following Christmas petition: 'Holy Father, in the town or borough of Usk, in the diocese of Llandaff, is a certain most honourable monastery of prioress and convent of nuns, under the profession of the order of St Benedict, who serve God with the greatest devoutness, which was of old endowed with sufficient possessions, rents and other profits; and in this monastery none but virgins of noble birth were and are wont to be received. But now, owing to the burnings, spoilings and other misfortunes which have been caused by the wars which raged in those parts, this monastery hath come to such want that unless ready help be found forthwith by your holiness, the sisterhood will be forced to beg for food and clothing, straying through the countryside, or to stay in the private houses of friends; whereby it is feared that scandals may belike arise. And seeing that within the walls of the same monastery there is built a certain chapel in honour of St Radegund . . . whereunto men of that country are wont to visit at certain festivals . . . now therefore prayeth your holiness your faithful chaplain and auditor, who first drew breath in the same town of Usk, that having pity with fatherly compassion on that monastery and prioress and nuns, you will deign graciously . . . to grant some indulgence, as your holiness thinks fit.'

And the Pope signed it thus: 'So be it as it is asked.'

It was custom in those times that any priest or suitable person making a pilgrimage to Rome at Easter, Whitsuntide or Christmas, and making a practical petition to the Pope, would have that petition granted. To have the chapel of St Radegund made a place of pilgrimage meant financial security to the nuns, who would benefit from the pilgrims boarding there, as well as from the offerings. Usk Priory still stands but is now a private house.

Goose Grease and Celluloid Dolls

ELIZABETH JARRET

Mrs Elizabeth Jarret is one of those timeless ladies – those unsung heroines who populate the less accessible areas of the countryside – who uncomplainingly 'get on with it'. In common with many of her generation, the prospect of toiling up two hundred feet of hillside from a distant bus stop, burdened with shopping, was just part of her apprenticeship as a young mother in the 1950s. Forty years ago, drivers around the many upland tracks and byways throughout the Marches would have to squint through rain-spattered windscreens at dimly lit hedgerows (no halogen headlamps in those days), taking care to avoid these hardy women, rarely brightly clad, routinely bringing to their hillside homes those elements of Christmas that were expected by their young families. Here a very philosophical lady tells of her 1930s childhood in Monmouth and compares it with her life some twenty years later as a mother of her own family on a hillside some five miles away from her childhood home.

I was an only child. That on its own was not enough to help balance the family budget. Despite there being fewer mouths to feed, we were very hard up in the 1930s: I think everyone was.

Christmas preparations began at school. Like most children I also went to Sunday school, so there were twice as many

preparations. I remember that we all made paper chains, but one thing particularly stands out in my mind. We used to go around the shoe shops trying to get old shoe boxes. We would line them with straw and put a dolly inside as baby Jesus. This would form part of a crib which we would decorate up just to suit ourselves.

All down Monnow Street the butcher's shops would have chickens, geese and turkeys hanging up outside for those last few days before Christmas. Lots of shops would put up decorations; it seemed more special then, somehow. It wasn't as glitzy as today, but just seemed nicer. I don't know if it really was much better, or whether it is just a child's view looking back.

At the bottom of Monnow Street there was a Christmas bazaar. I liked that: there were always lots of toys. Other shops would have special offers for Christmas. Most had some sort of Christmas club.

There was an outfitters in Church Street that had a club for school coats. My mum would put away about 6*d* (2.5p) per week for a new coat. She would say things like, 'You'll get a new coat for Christmas,' but I wasn't really bothered. The coat was for school. I would get the old one, though, for playing in. We didn't have lots of children's clothing then; it was only school uniform for best, or old school uniform for playing in if you didn't have smaller brothers or sisters.

There was always a school trip, and a Sunday school treat. The school trip was to the cinema, which is now closed down of course. There was a children's matinee, with Father Christmas, who would give us small presents of sweets and packets of peanuts and suchlike. The Sunday school treat was a party with lots of blancmange and jelly.

I used to go carol singing with my friends. We would put a candle in a jam jar as a lantern and go from door to door. Folks wouldn't let you get away with just one verse, they

would want to hear the whole thing through, and usually another one as well. We didn't always get money for singing, sometimes it was just sweets, nuts or mince pies.

In those days we used to have Midnight Mass in St Mary's Anglican Priory Church. As a girl I thought it was gorgeous. The choirboys carried candles around the church with all the other lights turned out. The singing made it a wonderful experience. Sadly they had to stop it a few years later as too many drunks started coming in from the pubs. I'm glad to see that they restarted it again a few years ago.

On Christmas morning the stockings always had the same sort of things in them. Always an orange in the toe. Also there would be a shiny penny, and sometimes a celluloid doll.

We weren't one of the wealthy families, so we couldn't afford goose at first. It was always chicken. In those days chicken was a treat, now it's no longer special, it's just an everyday thing. We had to have Brussels sprouts and roast potatoes with the chicken. It wouldn't have been a proper Christmas dinner without them.

Other members of the family would come round on Christmas Day, all bringing something. We would have about six in the house. We would have a small tree decorated with tinsel. The rest of the room would have paper chains and paper chinese lanterns hung around, and a little bit of holly and mistletoe hung up. The whole celebration was a family effort.

Of course when I got older, I was more interested in dressing up and meeting all my friends at the pub. That didn't last long, mind, as when I got married and had my own home, I had the help of the family to put on my own Christmas.

I only had Nicola, which meant that when I went shopping I didn't have as much to carry as some who lived up the hill. My husband had a motor-bike and sidecar which carried a lot of the Christmas shopping when he wasn't working.

I would cook a goose. That meant I had to get up early on Christmas morning, and make sure the range was banked up and hot. That goose would take most of the day to cook. My husband had a lot of relatives who would all do something different. Gerald Scotford next door had eight children. They would cook the Christmas pudding in the laundry copper!

Anyway, before everyone turned up, I would need some help to tip the pan with the goose on its side, and drain off the goose grease. There were gallons of the stuff! I would always keep it until it went off, in case Nicola had a cold. It was good for bruises too. I would rub it on her back or her front, depending on what was the problem. She didn't like it mind, going to play with her friends smelling of goose grease. It may have smelled, but it was a very useful by-product of the Christmas dinner!

The Orphans' Christmas

EUGENE COQUERAL

There is a popular misconception that the further one goes back,
the more miserable Christmas could be for the less fortunate.
The poem 'Christmas Day in the Workhouse' has impressed in
our minds an image of distress and institutional self-

righteousness. Eugene Coqueral, who now works as the archivist for St Mary's RC Church in Newport, knows all about institutional attitudes, having spent all his childhood Christmases in an orphanage, and suffering for many years from partial sight. Despite this, here he describes genuine efforts to brighten the Christmas season for unfortunate children, in the days before therapy and counselling became the panacea for all ills.

My father died in June 1941, two months before my birth. His death was not as a result of the war, it was just one of those things that happen. My mother was too young and immature to cope, so I was duly placed at Nazareth House in Cardiff. Within a few years I was transferred to Greytrees in Newport.

There was a real attempt there to get a family atmosphere going by having what are now called house mothers, but what were known then as assistants, under a matron. The assistants were always called 'Auntie', but Matron was always 'Matron'.

The build up to Christmas was gradual. The 'powers that be' were always afraid that we would become over-excited and uncontrollable. The first real signs that Christmas was really coming would be when the Red Cross, who came up to teach us various simple crafts, would start to show us how to make paper chains and paper lanterns. We never actually decorated the children's home with these decorations, as they were not up to a professional enough standard for when the various governors would visit us at Christmas time.

Unlike other children, we did not go Christmas shopping, again because they were afraid that we would either get over-excited or feel miserable seeing other children with their parents. Eventually, though, we would be taken for a very long walk into town to buy Matron a Christmas present. 'Auntie' would say beforehand, 'What do you think Matron

would like for Christmas?' If you were a bit frightened of her, or didn't really like her, you would get a packet of coloured bath salts for about a shilling (5p) and perhaps a tube of Spangles for any particular friends.

I remember the shop windows in Newport seemed to be better decorated than they are today; shop owners appeared to put a lot more effort into their displays. I don't remember there being lots of lights, but the displays of presents and snowy scenes always caught my fancy. I don't really know that they were better today in adult eyes, or whether it was such a treat to me that any old thing would have been wonderful. The thing was, we only got one trip into town, and we always seemed to hurry in order to get Matron her bath salts, and that was it until next year!

Matron and the assistants would start decorating a couple of days before Christmas, so that everything was in good order and tidy for the governors' visit. The Christmas tree would be put up and decorated mostly with paper garlands and some baubles. This would be covered up until Christmas Eve, so we wouldn't get over-excited. (They were always worried about 'over-excitement' in those days.) The tree would be standing in the corner of the dining room, covered over with a sheet, just a promise of what would be coming. I think we got excited anyway!

We were never allowed out on our own, so when I was twelve or thirteen I wanted very much to go to Midnight Mass. I was told that as there was no one to take me, I couldn't go. I wasn't having any of that, so the night before I opened a little-used window, then on Christmas Eve I sneaked down and hopped out. I enjoyed the mass, then got back undiscovered. I was not found out until I started boasting about it on Boxing Day. Someone snitched, and I was punished by losing my pocket money of 7s 6d (37.5p) per week for three weeks!

'Behind you!' A child of the 1970s enjoys the pantomime that
Eugene Coqueril in the 1930s had to watch in disciplined silence.

We had Christmas stockings (they were grey as far as I
recall); there wasn't very much in them, usually an apple, an
orange, a Mars Bar, and a Dinky Toy. The governors would
visit us on Christmas Day, bringing presents of pencils or
crayons and a colouring book, for example. We all were expected
to be seen enjoying ourselves.

We always had a good Christmas dinner, with crackers and
funny hats. The orphanage would always be given special
concessions and gifts from the various businesses in Newport.
I remember particularly that we always had a free ticket for
the swimming baths once a week or so. At Christmas we
would be given extra tickets, probably to cool us down in case
we became over-excited again.

We would be taken in a large group to the pantomime, which was a real treat for all of us. Even then we were discouraged from becoming 'over-excited'. We were allowed to clap, but we could not laugh or join in with shouts of 'Behind you!' or 'Oh no you haven't!' The actors were always puzzled by this group of solemn children, and would go out of their way to make us laugh. We wanted to, but we were afraid of upsetting Matron!

We were made aware of the fact that there were plenty of children in the world who were far worse off than us. It was for that reason we would never know exactly when Father Christmas would come. He had to visit all the poorly children in hospital first. Sometimes he would come on Boxing Day, which caused a lot of excitement and noise.

Boxing Day was always a happy and cheerful day, but New Year was for grown-ups only. The decorations would come down after New Year, then a sort of gloom would settle over us for a while as we faced another year of routine.

It was disadvantaged, but we made what we could of it. The staff were all doing their best, and in some ways we were an experiment in trying new techniques in bringing up orphans. It was not as bad as the 1920s and '30s when it was very institutionalized. We did feel that there was a real attempt to give some feeling for family life, in spite of problems with money, rules and a system.

The Grand Show – 1

*Many of the shops in the towns of Monmouthshire put on a
'Grand Show' for several weeks before Christmas. People
remember these windows with some nostalgia for times long
gone. The following extract is made up from over twenty
accounts of Christmas from the end of the nineteenth century up
to the 1950s.*

I remember when William Halls in Monmouth, where Boots
now is, would be the first to put up their Christmas Show in
Monnow Street. And what a display it was too. We used to
say, 'Best of all is William Hall's.'

They had big windows, which they used to pile high with
baskets of dried and sugared fruits and nuts – pyramids of
plum puddings, biscuits and cakes, Christmas crackers,
chocolates – all the things that as children we coveted. It was
enough to keep us standing gazing in the window for ages. In
fact some mothers would set their children outside the shop
to look at the show, while they went across the road to the
market stalls to do their shopping!

In the other window were all the bottles and kegs of strong
liquor. We were not bothered about these, though some of the
bolder boys would boast about whose dad could empty a keg
all by himself and still walk home.

All the main shops put on a show; we didn't need street
decorations, the shops were enough. About two weeks before
Christmas we were all clammering to be allowed to get the
bus into the local market towns to go look at the show. There

83

William Hall's elaborate
advertisement showing his stocks,
in readiness for the Grand
Christmas Show, early twentieth
century.

was one shop, Sterrets the bakers in St James Street, which
one special year (for me anyway) had a magnificent display of
Christmas wedding cakes. I had just got engaged, so my head
was filled with such fanciful notions of an all white wedding,
on an all white Christmas! Well I didn't get my white
Christmas, but I did get a Christmas wedding in 1924, and I
did get my wedding cake from Sterret's, complete with a
Christmas tree on it!

Another shop which managed to make a show out of very
ordinary everyday items was Stanley Gowers, who advertised
'A nice selection of most useful presents'. He sold such things
as eiderdowns, cushions, tea-cosies, aprons, gloves and
umbrellas, fancy linens and the like, so cleverly displayed and
decorated round that you wondered why you had not

considered such a shop for all your gift problems! What's more, Gowers had a catalogue, so you could go home and make up your mind in peace instead of trying to remember who you wanted to buy presents for in a crowded market day shop.

> *Bon Marché was a long-established shop remembered by the very oldest. A ladies' outfitters and haberdashers, with a chain of shops right across Monmouthshire, it had all the best French fashions, ribbons and trills. An advertisement was not sufficient for Bon Marché, but an editorial was considered more fitting, as this piece from the* Monmouthshire Beacon, *Christmas 1945 shows. (The piece was used many times before then, and repeated in several issues up to 1959 at least.)*

WOMEN AND CHRISTMAS The bowl of nuts, the dish of fruit and all the Christmas fare; the hangings, the trimmings, the holly and the mistletoe; the Christmas stockings, the preparations for visitors; the Yule log backed with coals to radiate its glowing warmth into the room; what a wealth of loving time, thought and loving care has been put into all these things by the woman of the house for the children – especially for the children – for the husband, for their relatives and friends and lastly for herself.

She plans ahead, saves ahead, works ahead, while the man, bless his carefree heart, is usually content to leave things until it is time for him to carve the turkey or pour the wines! So, you menfolk, do your best to lend a hand, and hand out the money, for don't dare to forget that Christmas can be an expensive time.

Expensive maybe, but not necessarily wasteful. Woman usually thrills to the thought of some costly but frivolous gift, but her practical nature always appreciates something to wear or use, always providing it is in a nice style and good quality.

Such items can be seen at Bon Marché, Church Street, Monmouth, in a variety such as: nylons, lingerie, housecoats, blouses, skirts, suits, dresses, swedette (sic) jackets, jumpers, cardigans, twinsets, bedjackets, gloves, wool and silk scarves, tablecloths, boxed towel sets, children's wear, party dresses, pram sets and everything for baby's comfort – rompers, suits, coats, shawls, etc.

YOU DO BEST at the friendly
BON MARCHÉ

The Grand Show – 2

MRS WYATT

Mrs Wyatt, who was an octogenarian in 1972, remembered the first Christmas that she was allowed to accompany her Mama and the maid for the Christmas shopping in Chepstow. She too refers to a 'Grand Show' and Bon Marché in this reminiscence full of fascinating detail.

I remember how proud I felt the year Mother, 'Mama' as we always called her, said that I might accompany her to the town to buy Christmas presents. We went in the covered chaise: it was a cold time, I remember, in 1898, and Annie, Mama's maid came with us to carry the parcels which could

not be delivered. I must have been, let me see, about ten years old I think, and I wore a red cashmere cape embroidered with cream silk embroidery from India, and had a little rabbit fur muff, with a special little purse compartment inside it where I kept my own Christmas money. I had 1*s* 9*d* (less than 10p in new money, but worth an awful lot to a child in those days!).

We went to a famous store popularly called the 'Golden Five Stores' (I don't know why). Their advertisements in the newspapers of their 'Grand Shows' were most enticing, selling all manner of things from sugarplums to perfumes – I got all of my Christmas presents there, some preserved ginger for Papa and Grandpapa, and a box of chocolate creams for Mama which cost a whole sixpence, but the man let me have something off, so I only paid fourpence and a halfpenny. With another fourpence halfpenny I bought a big box of crackers for the rest of our house visitors that year. I forget the design of them, the assistant said that they were 'very patriotic', and they were by Tom Smiths in London, who made crackers for the Queen, so I thought that they must be very good indeed. I did not yet know who was coming, so this seemed to me to be the best solution – though I think it was the nice Mr Thomas who ran the store who suggested it! I remember that the crackers each had a little flag inside of different nations we were friendly with, and soldier hats and crowns.

I so wanted to get Mama a bottle of the lovely French perfume. The bottles were cut glass with fancy stoppers, some were even banded with silver. But the very smallest would have cost me all of my pennies, without anything left for anyone else. Later, Mama said that she enjoyed the chocolates better anyway, because she only used one special scent and it would have been very sad if I had got the wrong one. I think she was just being nice because I was sure that I had smelt several different scents on her at different times!

Mama shopped there for a very long time, and I was kept occupied by Mr Thomas, who played games with me. We used to play games like 'I spy' and 'Minister's cat' and 'My Aunt Alice'. After Mama had finished her purchases we went to another shop called Bon Marché. This was a very fashionable shop where Mama always bought new French ribbons for her bonnets and to trim dresses. They also had a 'Grand Show' as I recall, with pretty gowns in the window for the party season. Mama wanted to buy a new fan for the ball the grown-ups would have at Christmas, as well as some other things. I was allowed to help choose the fan. There was a whole wall of highly polished wooden drawers, and the assistant opened two and brought them to the counter. There were fans of all kinds, ostrich feathers dyed all sorts of colours, painted kid, I cannot remember them all. But the one which drew my attention was high on a shelf displayed with a huge perfume bottle. It was a silky creamy lace on delicate ivory frets, and was the loveliest I had ever seen. The assistant said that it was 'Maltese lace', and one of the best they had, but with my persuasion – added to that, no doubt, of the assistant – Mama did buy it! I discovered later that she had bought some little French silk rosebuds to sew on my muff. They appeared in the top of my stocking, which we believed was filled by Father Christmas, but Mama explained that she had tiptoed in early in the morning and popped the little twist of tissue with the rosebuds in, on top.

We then had tea; I don't remember if we had tea in Bon Marché or not, but if not it was somewhere close by. The tea room was decorated with Chinese lanterns and was very pretty. I remember that we had a pot of tea in a silver pot, and a plate of tiny sandwiches followed by fruit cake for Mama and Annie, and an iced finger bun for me. Fruit cake was considered very bad for the digestion of children!

When we finally finished our shopping and went home, I hurried importantly to the nursery, where I hid my purchases until I could put them on the table by the big tree which we would have on Christmas Eve. It was a special Christmas because of the shopping.

Christmas in a Welsh Vicarage

IRENE FORD

Monmouthshire is home to both Welsh and English, as are most Border regions. This account recalls a childhood Christmas at a Church of England parish around the turn of the century.

Christmas Eve – when time stands still and the mystery of the first Christmas Eve is yearly reborn! It enveloped the eighteenth-century vicarage where my childhood was spent, as closely as did the magnificent beeches among which it lay.

Set back from the little-frequented roadway by a long drive, the house, once a farmhouse, waited with us for the coming of Christmas morning. The creaking of the old worn stairs answered our whispers as we crept up to bed with a lighted candle, whilst our elders, more on the fringe of the mystery, bustled about downstairs, doing all those things that

have to be done on Christmas Eve when the children have gone to bed. There was the rustling of paper as stockings were filled, the endless parading from room to room, and the enthusiastic stoking of the old kitchen range.

There were five of us, four girls and a boy. But in spite of that we managed to creep into bed without a sound, and we lay with closed eyes, ecstatically imbibing the delicious aroma of mince pies that wafted up to us from the kitchen. Occasionally one of us whispered to the others, 'Are you awake?' It was an unnecessary question. This night was never meant for sleep, especially as all five of us were allowed to crowd into two beds in this room at the front of the house for Christmas.

Slowly, slowly, the first hours of the night went by. At length the sounds downstairs ceased, and we heard the stealthy footsteps of the elders ascending the stairs, and the house slept . . .

In the night we felt for our stockings. I can still feel the squares and rounds of those black cashmere gym stockings, and how well I recall when my brother undid his stocking in the blackness, and an orange thudded on to the linoleum. It was as well that those old doors and walls were thick!

If only we could have known the time. But we dared not strike a match yet. We lay there absorbing the mystery of those waiting hours, saying very little, until we deemed it safe to light a candle and have a hurried look at the contents of our stockings. The scent of a tangerine still recalls the scene for me!

These, with apples, nuts and chocolates wrapped in a serviette, a few handkerchiefs, puzzles, crayons, snakes and ladders or ludo, generally filled the stockings. What magic imparted itself to these things to make them seem new and exciting every year? We gloated over them, ate a few chocolates and tried to put everything back in the stockings

before putting out the candle. It was not safe to keep it burning for long, showing a light under the door.

Satisfied, for the time being, by this excitement, we lay back contentedly for the next instalment.

The narrow lace curtains were never drawn across, and by sitting up in bed we could see the top of the hill leading down to the vicarage. But it was too soon to look yet. First would come the stirring sound of the ringing of the church bell at exactly 4 a.m. The sexton was exempt from duty on this occasion, and the bell would be rung by some half a dozen young men from the parish. How did they manage to ring it so wildly and yet not bring its half-ton weight crashing down from its roost in the Norman tower? There it was! We sat up in bed lest we should miss any of that wild clanging. Revellry, triumph and joy were in it!

From the moment when the last reverberating sound died away, time became real, prosaic. From that moment we could gauge roughly how long it would take those young men to run from the church to the sexton's house, and hurriedly swallow bacon and eggs. Our house would be their next destination.

Now our eyes were glued on the hill, watching, waiting. There it was at last; the flickering light of a torch. It moved quickly down the hill and became lost in the hollow. Then the voices, gruff ones, hearty ones. We hugged our knees, waiting for the click of the gate. That was it! And now came the crunching of heavy feet on the drive. That was our signal. With one accord, we dived out of bed and rushed to the window, flinging up the bottom and then standing back a little.

The footsteps came to a halt at the front of the house. Then came a short pause before a unisoned 'Merry Christmas, Vicar.'

We never heard Father's reply. I doubt if he did answer! We were all 'the Vicar', shouting loudly, 'Thank you, the same to you.'

There was the maid unbarring the front door!

Hurriedly we dragged on our clothes, poured icy water into the basin on the washstand and splashed our faces. Then we were rushing loudly, madly down the stairs.

How wonderful the coffee smelt and the mince pies! Could they ever taste as good as at four o'clock on Christmas morning? What a chattering there was too! The noise might have been less had Father been there, but he was still in bed, trying to fortify himself with sleep for quite a long test of endurance.

Now the coffee pots were empty, and the stack of mince pies sadly depleted. The young men duly full, I imagine, of bacon, eggs, coffee and mince pies, got up to go and rouse the sleepy members of their own households. We for our part were obliged to sit down quietly until a quarter to six, when we all set out to walk the quarter mile to church for the main service of the day, which began at 6 a.m.

Trotting along the lonely road in the darkness, yawning occasionally after our long vigil, we pressed on until we came to the top of the hill. From that point we could view, in the hollow of the village, the friendly glow in the windows of the oil-lit church, the relatively dim light seeming bright against the blackness outside.

We sang our way through most of the two-hour service, and it was with a feeling almost of disenchantment that we trooped out into the early daylight when it was over. There was another to follow at 11 a.m., but that would be without the thrill of the 'Plygain' (literally, 'Cockcrow'), as the early service was called.

So it was for us that from daylight onwards the day took on the pattern of all Christmas days, and the pattern that my own children know. Not for them, on Christmas Eve, in this fashionable town where we live, the utter stillness of a country night, and the excitement of footsteps on a long gravel path.

Nor have they heard an old bell exploding into the night, scattering into the air the miracle of all Christmases; or known the ambrosial taste of coffee at half past four in the morning. These joys were mine, and the nostalgic memory of them returns every year. I can close my eyes and see, not a brightly lit street, but a lonely road leading down to an old, old house, a house with shutters and lace curtains, a house that knows how to be still, to wait and to welcome.

Did it Snow?

COUNT ANDRZEJ VON STAUFER

Many old people will tell you that Christmases were snowy when they were children. What are the facts? This was highly unlikely in Monmouthshire as, bounded on its southern side by the Bristol Channel, the influence of the Gulf Atlantic Drift would ensure that the climate was milder there than in East Anglia which is on the same latitude. No part of Monmouthshire is further than fifty miles (as the cloud drifts) from the sea. There is no shortage of high ground, however, with several areas rising to more than two thousand feet. Typically snow will lie above fifteen hundred feet on a cold winter day when the temperature is at 3 °C on the coastal plain. Sea temperatures rarely drop below 4 °C, which will always provide a warming, often foggy effect on cold days in the vicinity of Newport.

Frosty days are far more common. In areas of the Wye and Usk valleys, local inhabitants may often see white Christmases caused by hoar frost after a night of freezing fog. This may well have led to a memory of 'white Christmases' when no snow has been recorded.

A northerly airstream is required to bring cold, moisture-laden air necessary for snowfall. Unfortunately for Monmouthshire, this air has already crossed Scotland, Cumbria and Wales, depositing its load on every mountain in its way before reaching the county. It takes a rare combination of circumstances to bring about real snowfall in any quantity. As the data below will show, the occasions when a polar low form over Monmouthshire during the festive season are very uncommon.

There are no synoptic reporting stations in Monmouthshire, Ross-on-Wye being the nearest, some seven miles from the County March. Bristol and Rhoose are the next nearest, but they both give a representative sample of the coastal weather environment. Inferences have been drawn from these local reports and the vertical temperature profile as understood at the time. By the time the exceptional blizzards of Boxing Day 1962 had arrived, forecasts had improved little since the wartime standard of accuracy available in 1947. Contrary to popular memory, that winter gave us snowfall in March, and not at Christmas time. Memories are at fault here, not the forecasts!

Christmases 1939–50
1939 Following a wet start to December, Monmouthshire enjoyed a period of relative dryness. Some snow fell on the highest ground in the north of the county, but did not lie for any great duration. By the time that Christmas preparations would have been well under way during the second week of the month, it had become markedly colder. Snow showers became more frequent, but they were not heavy and caused

little problem. Freezing fog, however, was a major factor for Christmas week, giving way briefly to a period of fine frosty days before returning in time for New Year.

1940 December began unusually dry, with little rain at a season where it is regarded as the norm. By the second week it had become particularly cold, with freezing fog on occasions. It rained in time for Christmas, then gave way to a particularly cold spell, with some local snow at higher levels just after Christmas.

1941 December was by and large a balmy month, with temperatures more in keeping with the Mediterranean than Wales. There was some local fog, particularly in sheltered valleys. Fortunately for Monmouthshire, winds kept the worst of the fog away. Boxing Day saw a little bit of snow on high ground as the weather turned very cold immediately after Christmas Day.

1942 Gales marked the greater part of the month, with severe problems for shipping in the Bristol Channel. Many reports were received of considerable storm damage. Monmouthshire was spared the dense fogs that affected the Clyde Valley and London on Christmas Day, causing several deaths. Snow was observed, however, even at low level between Christmas Day and New Year.

1943 After a rainy start, frost had settled over the county by the second week. The run in to Christmas Day, however, was marked by unseasonal thunderstorms. Snow was not seen at all in the county either before or after Christmas.

1944 December was a very cold month. Wintry showers were frequent, but the air was unstable, giving mixtures of hail, sleet and thunderstorms. Despite the cold, little snow was seen. The abiding memory of this Christmas was dense, blanketing and freezing fog in the industrial valleys.

1945 The first Christmas of peace had been preceded by a very unsettled and rainy few weeks. Rain was particularly

heavy on Christmas Eve, but snow arrived, albeit briefly, just after Christmas, with some very wet but heavy falls.

1946 Once again the prospects for a white Christmas were drowned out by persistent rain. Children's hearts may have been raised by a brief cold spell just before Christmas. The feast itself was very mild indeed, almost warm, recording temperatures more in keeping with Easter.

1947 An early cold spell was followed by very mild dull weather. Newport and Usk enter the record books with temperatures of 58 °F on 20 and 24 December. By Christmas Day it had been raining hard.

1948 The whole month looked as if it was going to be very mild and unsettled, but there was a gradual change to colder frosty weather. It was in no sense a white Christmas, until considerable snow fell at all levels on 30 December.

1949 When it began to snow on 10–11 December, one could be forgiven for anticipating a white Christmas. This was not to be: temperatures rose steadily, with substantial rain over the Christmas holiday.

1950 This year there was very nearly a white Christmas over the whole county. Snow fell for twenty days in December at Bwlchgwyn, with considerable snowfalls being experienced on many rural roads. Christmas Day was cold, and many of the higher hill farms would certainly have had a real white Christmas.

And the coldest of them all?

December 1962 was a very cold month. Few places in Monmouthshire would have enjoyed temperatures above freezing at any point from the second week of December. Christmas Day itself would have had a maximum anywhere of −2 °C, many places being much colder than that. The ground was like iron, and was to be so for another three months.

Small birds deserted the area, heading for the warmer climes of the Devon and Cornwall coasts. Water mains froze, and an expected thaw on 26 December brought instead freezing rain which caused major traffic chaos, followed by blizzards. Little did the good citizens of Monmouthshire realize that they were about to undergo a Siberian winter on a scale that had not been experienced since the seventeenth century!

Snow

MYFANWY HAYCOCK

This poem is taken from a book of old Monmouthshire verse.
Nothing is known of the author.

When twilight faded greyly gold
As withered daffodils,
A million million frosty sheep
Came flocking from the hills.

By woolley ones and tattered twos,
And threadbare threes they came,
And all of them were similar,
Yet no two were the same.

We didn't hear them coming,
Nor did we see them go,

A Monmouthshire Christmas

Snow over Monmouthshire.

We only saw when morning came,
Their wool as soft as snow.

White tangled on the hedges
And strewn on fields and hills,
Beneath a sky still greyly gold
As withered daffodils.

And surely someone must have found
It hard to fall asleep –
That he should have to count and count
A million million sheep.

How it all Changed

REG LIVESEY

*It has been a truism to say that Welsh families and customs
held on in the hill farms and industrial valleys, while the
English settled the farming lowlands. Over much of
Monmouthshire and the earlier kingdom of Gwent, there has
been a constant flux of cultural invasion. Since the Industrial
Revolution the boom town mentality of the incoming Irish and
English immigrants swamped any Welsh Christmas customs
that may have survived in the industrial valleys. What is not
so well known is the Agricultural Revolution which displaced
whole upland rural Welsh communities. Reg Livesey, a
founder of the Gwent Rural Life Museum, was an unwitting
herald of change in the uplands of north Monmouthshire, as
he now explains.*

I was born well before the First World War, and had always
been brought up with the idea of England, Wales and
Monmouthshire; so when my brother went to manage an
upland farm in 1926, from where we lived in Lancashire, it
didn't seem as if he was going to Wales.

I joined him from agricultural college as a pupil in the
following year. Around then a farming assistant would earn
about five shillings a week (25p). I did not learn an awful lot
about farming, being a heaver and shifter, so I left to join a
commercial firm as a fitter installing milking machines, where
I learned a great deal more about modern efficient farming.

There were many changes being made throughout the twenties and the thirties. Small farms were being sold up and amalgamated with larger concerns. It was becoming possible to farm on ever higher land. A marginal farm would probably be ploughed from top to bottom, winning pasture from bracken and heather at altitudes of up to fifteen hundred feet. Above that it would be hill farm sheep country only.

Many of the smaller farmers were tenants farming very inefficiently, reliant upon a large labour force, and with low profitability. These must have been the old Welsh communities with their own customs. They probably had to sit out the bad winter weather, and therefore had time to celebrate Christmas in a traditional way.

When I took over the management of the farm in 1942, the War Executive Committee were buying up smaller hill farms, then releasing these as larger parcels of land to existing farmers in order to produce more food for the war effort. Most of the younger men were called up, while their parents' generation often retired, or at any rate left the area.

Even in a cold winter (we had several of those throughout the 1940s) you could not slack off at all. There was no cheery day off with a rosy-cheeked farmer's wife providing Christmas dinner for all the labourers. I probably had about four men full time who would just work until the job was done, then go home. I never had a Christmas dinner in the middle of the day, work came first. Usually everyone was too tired to celebrate much.

A typical 1940s Christmas season would run like this. The mangolds would have been put in clamps as fodder for the livestock by the beginning of December. Throughout the beginning of the month the winter kale was cut and hauled, and the turnips would have been harvested. It was a matter of national concern that root vegetables and potatoes were reliably stored, as food was rationed. The first concern was

feeding the nation (the national cry was 'Don't you know there's a war on?'). No one had turkeys: you got boiling fowl if you were lucky.

When Christmas Day dawned, the milking would have already been done. White Christmases were dreaded, as the milk had to be got away to the dairies. My farm was 450 feet above sea level at its lowest, rising to 1,384 feet, so snow on the top was not uncommon.

The rest of the day would have been spent in feeding the animals, and bringing down any sheep that had been caught out by severe weather. Many of the ewes were in lamb at that time of year, and you could not afford to take risks. One severe winter we seemed to spend our time digging the ewes out, and trying to get the milk down to the village. I remember when drifts blocked the roads, and we could not get the milk out for three or four days. If it froze in either tank or churn, it was no good. Christmas was if anything a time of worry.

During severe weather I could only get around in my Fordson Major half track; I later had a tracked Morris Bren Carrier which was very useful in the snow.

Working so hard, one didn't tend to notice if the workers were English or Welsh, all that mattered was if they got the work done. Apart from a Christmas dinner at the end of the day, you could have missed Christmas entirely. Life was very hard for everyone. There would not have been a lot to spend, as the farm workers would get 48 shillings (£2.40) per week.

As I say, I never got to hear of any customs when we were working, as we were all too busy. Remember, this was one English managed farm covering what would have been half a dozen Welsh hill farms: their way of life had gone when they had been bought out. Our job was to produce as much as possible from the smallest area at the lowest cost. The demands of the war effort, and subsequent commercial pressures, killed for good the old slow rural life.

Christmas Day in Chepstow Workhouse

This article appeared in the Chepstow Weekly Advertiser, *3 January 1891. By the 1930s Chepstow Workhouse had become an infirmary.*

Christmas Day at Chepstow Workhouse was befittingly opened by Divine Service in the morning at which the chaplain officiated. But the Christmas dinner was, no doubt, to the inmates, the chief business of the day. The Master and Matron, Mr T.V. and Miss Steel, had tastefully decorated the dining hall for the occasion, and they and their staff had a busy time of it during the morning in preparing the dinner, which was laid on table about one o'clock.

Each able bodied person was supplied with ½ lb prime beef and their platters piled up with potatoes and parsnips, which was followed by a supply of plum pudding of excellent quality, washed down, by the adults who were not teetotal, with an allowance of ale.

The occupants of the sick wards were also looked after, and came in for their share of good things. The kindly hearted Master and Matron were assiduous in looking after those in their charge, and it was a gratifying sight to see the way in

which the poor people, who all looked clean and comfortable, enjoyed their Christmas fare.

The beneficient lady of St Pierre, Mrs Lewis, sent, for the delectation of the old people, a quantity of tea and sugar, and Dr King the medical officer kindly contributed a quantity of oranges.

Christmas in St Arvans

JOYCE EDMONDS

Local historian Joyce Edmonds has done much to collect the stories of the old families of Monmouthshire in her two books, Tales of Old St Arvans *and* Tales of the Llanishen Parishes. *In the first extract she interviews Arthur Selway of the St Arvans Selway family, who remembers how he began work and ended up in the RAF during the Second World War.*

I started at St Arvans School when five years old and left at fourteen years. Mr Tom Williams was headmaster. I enjoyed the sports days. These were held on the playing field behind the school, or on the lawns of Wyndcliffe Court. Mrs Alice Williams took us to the Beachley Pool for swimming lessons.

Out of school, not only did we play Fox and hounds but also Kick the can. To play this a chosen person had to hide,

and then get back and kick the can before being caught. Stones were put in the can to make more noise. We used to swim in the trout pool in the Brake, up on the hill.

I trained in the grocery trade in Chepstow. Each Christmas, a crowd of us would go round carol singing to get some extra money. The first Christmas of the war, when I was sixteen, we were singing outside the Wyndcliffe Court and Freda slipped out to join us. She was about my age, and personal maid to Bridget, sister of Mrs Patrick Clay (Mrs Scott). We all knew that us boys would have to go to the war very soon and it was a rather special occasion. We ended up at Mrs Phillips' house at No. 1 The Row. She had a piano and would play for us. The front room was crowded and there was no room for Freda to sit. Mrs Phillips said, 'Go and sit on Arthur's knee,' and she did.

Freda and I were buying sweets in the post office. Mr Sunderland suggested that I join the Home Guard. Mr Tom Williams had been a captain in the 1914/18 war and he was organizing it. I was not there long because I volunteered for the Air Force. I was one of the first of the village boys to go. I was in the RAF by April 1941, and sailed from Glasgow on December 9th of that year.

Another memory (source now lost) from some twenty years before:

Before the war, Mrs Peglar of the Mount used to provide a Sunday school treat at Christmas. It was held in the memorial hall. Mrs Peglar would arrive alone in her own Rolls Royce. The treat was a slap-up tea and we were given presents suitable to our age group. One year I was in hospital with peritonitis and could not attend. I was given my present, though, a Rainbow Annual. I looked after that! I wrote in it. 'Black as a raven, black as a rook, black is the thief that steals this book.'

Carolling Gaily

GWYNNETH SUNDERLAND

*The Sunderland family played a large part in St Arvans life.
Mr Donald Sunderland was in charge of what was then called
'Electrics' (forty years ago St Arvans was the only village the
Monmouth side of Chepstow that had electricity). Here is
another extract from Mrs Edmonds's book,* Tales of Old St
Arvans, *written by his wife, Gwynneth, which paints a
wonderful picture of local life.*

Never was the gaiety of the village more apparent than in the
1960s when the carol choir came into its own. The young
people gladly joined the older villagers, and their voices
added a certain brightness and sparkle.

Mr Lewis the headmaster was the driving force behind it.
Mrs Kit Thomas, my mother, was appointed choirmaster. She
controlled us with the aid of a baton belonging to her brother
who had won it at an Eisteddfod. November saw the start of
the rehearsals which were held in the village school.

The sopranos, of course, were quite strong, a few contraltos
(myself and Joyce Edmonds included) were able to hold their
own. But alas! the gentlemen were a little backward in
coming forward. It was with some difficulty that we were able
to teach them the tenor and bass parts. I remember one dear
old soul no longer with us who declared that 'the bass part
was the same in all carols'! We certainly worked hard at
rehearsals. The homemade lemonade provided by Jenny

Junior carollers, Monmouth.

Lewis, the headmaster's wife, was pure nectar to our tired throats and did us a power of good.

My husband Donald played his piano accordian when we sang around the village streets. Hip flasks were the order of the day to keep the cold out on snowy, freezing, foggy and, yes, sometimes beautiful moonlight nights. One bitter evening, probably the coldest we had ever encountered, Don's face turned ashen, his hands turned blue and his fingers were so cold he could not feel them. Even the accordian froze up and was adorned with icicles.

Drinks were offered in profusion in the numerous big houses to which we were invited. We travelled as far as the 'Cayo' on the Newport Road, to 'St Annes' at Crossway Green and 'Gaer Hill' in St Arvans. Also 'Oakgrove' by the racecourse and 'The Glyn' in Itton, home of Mr Mahoney-Meade the Master of Foxhounds for the Curre Hunt.

Most of our hosts considered the visits of the carol singers part of the Christmas festivities and invited friends and relations to join them.

One regular visit was to the home of Nancy Bull at the Laurels Farm. She made delicious wines. These were much enjoyed by us all and on one occasion inspired us to sing 'Ding Dong Merrily on High' as it has never been sung before!

It was at Gaer Hill Farm (the second big house to be visited that night) that I, who played the piano, saw both the piano and the keys dancing around for the first time!

I did not drink much alcohol at that time, but drank from the glass that was put on the piano for me. I found it a pleasant drink and had a second. All was explained when I heard Joan Neal call out 'Mr Miles – you've opened up the best whisky.' (Mr Miles was the farmer.)

We had another big house to visit that night – Wyndcliffe Court, where Mr and Mrs Pat Clay were entertaining some Australian guests. It happened to be snowing – something the visitors had never seen. It was a lovely way to end the evening!

We often had red noses, even though clad in the warmest clothing. But the singing went on, for although the enjoyment was immense, the whole point of the singing was to raise money for charity. This we did to the tune of several hundred pounds (a lot of money in those days). The old pensioners in the village were usually given ten shillings (50p) each.

Neither did we forget the true meaning of Christmas in all the fun and laughter. We were able to fill both St Arvans and Itton churches for memorable carol services.

Oh yes, those were happy days. Fondly remembered by many people today.

Devil up the Drainpipe

REVD FATHER DAVID SMITH

Father David Smith, a convert to Catholicism, is now the parish priest for St Mary's in Monmouth, Wales's oldest post-Reformation Catholic church. His boyhood was spent in the industrial village of Blaenavon, during the post-war years when 'King Coal' was beginning its inexorable decline. Here he describes the carefree existence of children anticipating Christmas, unaware of the worries and privations endured by their elders as their way of life started to accelerate away from industrial security, towards the uncertainties of the modern consumer society.

Childhood in Blaenavon was a stress-free thing. Little things meant a lot. We all looked forward to the annual Sunday school outing to Barry Island as if it was the best thing in the world. Now recently I met a child who was bored with Disneyworld in Florida! That would have been a present from Heaven above for us.

Going back to school in September was a major blot on our horizon. The days grew shorter, and the mist would appear on the mountain and seemed to creep ever lower down the valley as the year advanced.

A Monmouthshire Christmas

The first real signs of Christmas were when choir practice included Christmas carols or even snatches of oratorio in school. Carol services would always be 'posh'. I don't know where they got the music from, but the repertoire was always very ambitious, with Schubert and Brahms being arranged and rearranged around the words for popular carols. I remember that Dorothy Adams Jeremiah was the musical director for Monmouthshire, so the standard had to be very high indeed.

A bit later in the term, we all started cutting out paper chains and paper lanterns. Some would be used in school, while others would find their way home. It always was paper decorations, not lots of foil and tinsel such as we have today. The paper lanterns were probably quite deadly once a lit candle had been placed within. We didn't care about safety, life was secure.

Life was so secure, in fact, that we would play out until way after dark, roaming up and down Coity Mountain. There was no fear of child molesters or abduction in those days. Your biggest fear was a clip round the ear, not always from your mother either.

We had a couple of mischievous games that we would play when we broke up for Christmas. One was called 'Knock down Ginger'. That often resulted in a clip round the ear if we were caught. The rules of the game were simple. You knocked on a door then ran away. The young menfolk particularly would run like mad to catch you. You had to be very quick indeed not to be caught and get a good clip. It was all part of the game. You didn't go home and tell your Ma as children do today. You just kept quiet and hope that the victim didn't tell your parents. There was none of this silly political correctness about child psychology that we have today. I don't think we were scarred by the experience!

The other mischief game was a real demon. It was called 'Devil up the drainpipe'. It was great! You needed some

newspaper and some matches. The drainpipes came attached to the houses, with obliging little spouts just above street level. The game was simple. You just stuffed some paper up the drainpipe, then lit it. The flames would draw straightaway, making a roaring noise that you could hear clearly in the house. We thought this game was very spectacular.

Children didn't go Christmas shopping, your mothers and aunties saw to that, coming back from the buses down the valley with lots of bags which didn't get opened. The men took no part in this. They would just bring home their paypackets unopened and hand them to their wives. If a husband had opened his paypacket, then something was seriously wrong. Men ruled the roost, but the community was a matriarchy!

As my father had been struck down by meningitis, all the work fell to my mother. Other members of the family would help out. This was not unusual at all, you needed the support of an extended family to get things done in difficult times. Everybody took that for granted.

Today coal fires are considered a bit of a nuisance. We always had coal fires – it was lovely. You could see the smoke from up the mountain, and when you came in, it always seemed warm and friendly. Auntie Gwyneth would always be singing, sometimes whole airs from the *Messiah*, with Auntie Gladys joining in – they had a fine pair of voices.

Auntie Gladys would always stuff the chicken, or later the turkey. I don't really know why my mother wouldn't do it. I remember it always seemed to be either the *Messiah* or *Amahl and the Night Visitors* every year on the radio, and I think it continued on the TV when it arrived in 1953. People would call on families who had TV just to see it. I think the first TVs had been bought to see the Coronation.

I think that everything was bought for Christmas at the Co-op: the 'divvy' (dividend stamp) was a major consideration. You tried to save in as many ways as possible.

Most families were members of some kind of Christmas club or another, putting away small sums of money for a Christmas treat.

You wouldn't see any electric fairy lights at all in the village. All the Christmas lights were candle or nightlight powered. I think they were nicer. We used to make our own lanterns for carol singing from an old jam jar and a Heinz baked bean tin. (It had to be Heinz in order to be the right size.) We would fill a jam jar with boiling water to knock the bottom out. After that we would screw the lid back on, place a nightlight on the inside on top of the lid. The baked bean can would have lots of holes punched in it, and the jagged opening (done with the old-style tin openers) would be jammed on top, making a kind of miner's-pattern carolling lamp. You had to use wire, not string, to hold the lantern. It always seemed cold and frosty when we went carol singing. Mind you, the village was above a thousand feet. Payment would be in pennies or sometimes sweets.

The Christmas tree would come in a couple of days before Christmas Eve. Mothers used to shoo their children outside the whole time so they wouldn't get too excited. Decorations were always paper, festooned all over the tree. It must have been terribly dangerous with all the candles, but I don't remember any fires.

When we went to bed on Christmas Eve, we were always too excited to sleep. My brother would convince me that I could just about hear sleighbells as Father Christmas arrived at our village.

We would be up very early to empty our stockings. The toys were simple, sometimes home-made from wood. One time I had a wooden train, but my brother demolished it with a hammer on Christmas afternoon!

We would all go early to church, then on to visit friends throughout the day. I would always visit school friends or

Sunday school friends and later on youth club friends as all the social activities were local. The men would go and visit their friends, often drinking home-made wine which was really very potent. When my grandparents were alive we would also go and visit them.

Eventually we would all go home for a late Christmas dinner with all the trimmings. That could go on until late in the evening. We knew how to enjoy ourselves as we were unsophisticated, taking pleasure in little things. I believed that the chapel people didn't celebrate Christmas at all, as it was too much sinful fun!

Boxing Day was really a day for the men. They would go to the pub, and the married men would play the unmarried men at darts, and there would also be a married versus single Rugby match about that time, maybe a day or two later. It was a very traditional custom.

Come New Year, the evening was an occasion for grown-ups, as they always drank each other's health for the coming year. It was very important to have a dark stranger call for good luck. There was one chap who lived down the road who was dark and had very black hair: he was always the first caller.

After that it would all fizzle out, and we dreaded going back to school. The holidays never seemed long enough!

I Remember a Christmas . . .

Talking about Christmas sparks off many memories. Sometimes only a sentence or two is required, as these reminiscences sent into the South Wales Argus *show. Together they paint a picture of domestic Christmas of decades past.*

I remember when you couldn't walk along here for the charabancs. It was just on the border see, just outside Wales, which was dry on Sundays and holy days. So Christmas Day brought out all the Welshmen in them charabancs, even on bicycles, queuing along the road here to the Crown for a drink! (Mr Pinches, Whitchurch)

There was always a nativity play – every school, nursery school and Sunday school had one. They seemed to become popular after the war, in the 1950s, and right into the 1980s, I don't know if they still do them. I can remember being involved with various volunteer groups, and with my own children, and one year attending, as a result, five nativity plays, including one done by the Mitchel Troy Infants School, one by Raglan Juniors and one by Redbrook with lovely hobby-horse style camels! (Miss Jameson, Abergavenny)

There used to be a Whitchurch Pantomime Society which put on a very good panto every year. One year they did *Aladdin*, with the Iris Cole School of Dancing – that was in 1952. It was so good that it was repeated at the Rolls Hall in

Above: Redbrook nativity play, complete with hobby-camels, mid-1970s. Below: Joan Walby played Aladdin in the Whitchurch pantomime, 1952. It later travelled to the Rolls Hall, Monmouth.

Monmouth — quite a compliment. Jean Walby played the principal boy, Aladdin, and Audrey Pugh was the Princess, with Kenneth Round as Widow Twanky and another local name, Frederick Lindsey, as the wicked Abanazar.

Now they have community carols round the village Christmas tree. We are in Herefordshire — postcode-wise anyway — but we live nearer to Monmouth, and there's The Forest just up the road the other way, which is Gloucestershire, a tiny triangle on a bend in the river between the counties. (Kingfisher Cruises, Symonds Yat)

Christmas for myself, brother and sister was a wonderful time. My mother would start the pudding five weeks before Christmas. Plenty of mixed fruit, suet and stout for mixing. For boiling the pudding we had a large copper boiler in the wash-house. My brothers used to stay up all night to keep adding water as it boiled. Mam would buy them some sweets and comics to keep them awake, and three candles for light. They loved that job.

For our Christmas stocking, my sisters and I had a piece of hair ribbon, a wooden pencil case, and Mam would put away some money on a club card in the sweet shop for an annual and a Cadbury selection box for each of us. My brothers would have marbles, whip and top, and one would have a hoop until one year my brother left it on the floor and my Dad stood on the end of it and it came up and hit him in the face! What he called Santa was nobody's business! On Christmas morning we were allowed a candle, as we had no electric light then. No turkey for dinner, only a small chicken. Mam and Dad had a leg each and we kids were lucky if we got a wing. We kids saved our pennies for a big bar of Cadbury's chocolate for Mum, and an ounce of Digger flake tobacco for Dad's pipe — a rare treat. It was rather a meagre time, but I am sure there were no happier children. (Mrs W. Gregory, Cwmbran)

Boiling the Christmas pudding in a laundry copper. The clock in
this early Victorian engraving, pictured at ten to six on Christmas
Eve, shows how long the process would have taken.

I have wonderful memories of Christmas past. Being the eldest of five children I had to help out a lot. My father was in poor health, so my mum had to go out to work. In fact she had quite a few jobs at Christmas time, including dressing chickens by the hundred for local farmers until her fingers bled.

My father made a lot of our toys, and I can remember him sending my brothers out on very cold winter's nights, to the banks of the River Ebbw, at Maesglas, to make coal balls for the fire from the dust washed down from the mines.

We only ever had a roast chicken for Christmas Day. Did we feel deprived and hard up? We did not. I have nothing but praise for my hard-working mother and father. (Lilian Kenvyn, Cwmbran)

Christmas time in our home would keep us busy making paper chains and collecting silver paper to decorate the holly tree. Four fatherless children in the 1930s, with mother taking in washing, you had to make the best of things. We would gather fallen logs from Cefn Wood. We'd help distemper the living room, and when it was still wet, make patterns on the wall with a potato cut in half. My Mam would rustle up a Christmas pud of some sort, and get that steaming. Rabbit was the meal of the day, but I do remember chicken once.

My joy was the Sally Army band playing in the street: we would form a ring and all sing carols. My sisters and I would give a turn each at singing and dancing, and my Mam would laugh until she cried and say you must never forget the true meaning of Christmas, and always keep your faith. (Mrs Molly Johnson, High Cross)

My earliest memory of Christmas is of when I was about three or four. Two days before Christmas Eve we set out from home; the snow was deep and hard, and I remember the lovely crunch crunch of our footsteps. As we neared the top of Broad

Street with the gas lamps throwing a glare on to Rutter's shop, what a sight! Rabbits and hares suspended over the windows, beautiful birds with glossy plumage, fir trees, great bunches of holly, mistletoe, sacks of oranges, apples with glossy skins, baskets of nuts, piles of huge onions, carrots and potatoes.

There was a hawker selling little tin monkeys on a stick and one was given to me. I remember the crowd of people all seeming to know one another in great good humour. Walking home, all carrying bags of exciting purchases, I was lifted up by a strong pair of arms, still clutching my tin monkey in my frozen hand. As I drifted off to sleep I could hear in the distance church bells. (Mrs D.E. Lucas, Aberyschan)

I remember as a little girl in the 1930s, fetching a jug of 'old beer' from the back door of the pub (used to mix the Christmas puddings), and my mother rising early to light the boiler fire as the puddings (about ten of them) boiled all day.

Our beef (salted, about 15 lb) was also boiled in the wash-house boiler, then left to cool. One Christmas our dog decided it had cooled enough and ate the lot! (Mrs V. Mayo, Caldicot)

I don't ever remember a tree or trimmings in my home at Christmas. My Mam died when I was only four, and I was the only child. My Dad did his best filling up the stocking but there was very little else. But I had a wonderful Santa, every year. It was the rentman who owned our house. Every Christmas when he collected the rent there was a beautiful present. A lovely baby doll one year, a beautiful china doll with eyebrows and lashes and eyes that opened and closed. Teddy bears, piano, tea sets, something every year from Mr James, a landlord turned Santa every Christmas. (Mrs J. Short, Aberbeeg)

Christmas at the Jenkins

JEN CHAMBERLAIN

Mrs Jen Chamberlain, wife of a local sheep farmer and builder, remembers her own childhood Christmases of the 1950s with fondness.

We always had a huge Christmas tree, right up to the ceiling, and all the presents were piled up underneath it. Uncle Henry always dressed up to play the part of Father Christmas, and hand out to each of us the 'Big Present'.

There was a big cupboard alongside the chimney in the parlour. Father Christmas used to come out of this cupboard, and we never knew how he did it, we always thought there must be a way into the chimney.

Carol, my sister, and I believed in Father Christmas until we were quite old. Until one morning I woke up, and there was Dad in my bedroom with 'the Sack'. I don't know who was more surprised, him or me!

There was always a huge bunch of mistletoe hung up, and holly everywhere in the house. It was easy in the country to get evergreens then. We had a big ten-setting farm table, and we used to have the whole family for Christmas dinner, all sitting round this huge table, with an enormous turkey, brown, crisp and succulent, in the place of honour in the middle.

We had my Nana living with us for fifteen years, and even though rules were rules, there was much love in our house,

and we used to have such a lovely Christmas. Not like today's commercial ones, and we didn't have all that amount of money to spend, but maybe it was better for that. We put more of ourselves and love into making a good Christmas.

I remember Dad used to go out and feed the animals early, so that he would have time with us children before we went to bed – very excited!

Uncle Harry used to be a Scout commander, so we used to play games – real games – all afternoon, not sit in front of the television like today's children. And we used to have prizes, so much more fun than nowadays. We were tired out after the games, so slept better for it.

Memories of Christmas

MARIJAN HUBERT

This poem is reprinted from Out of Hearing, *Taliesin Poetry Book (Monmouth Comprehensive School, 1994).*

Asleep – no, not asleep,
pretending to sleep.
Upstairs the attic window is,
as always, open to the night.
Snuggled down in warm quilts,

A Monmouthshire Christmas

looking at patterns made on
the wall by passing cars and
festive street lights.

The wind whistles – was it
the wind? or was it the chiming
of sleigh bells?
Yes, that's right, sleigh bells.
The lights on the landing
chase round a circuit,
like fairies dancing.
That's what these lights
really were: silver fairies
twirling with anticipation,
waiting for the Child's birth.

Creaks on the stairs.
Eyes close.
Heart pounds.

Cinnamon and saffron waft
through the room.
Nice smells.
Comforting smells.
Something is put
on the end of the pillow.
More creaks.
Other sounds,
exciting sounds.

The bedroom door squeaks shut.
Much too much excitement to sleep.
My last thought, as I drift on
warm waters to that place of
magic, that is a child's dreams.

Christmas Shopping

Being the county town of the shire, Monmouth was the centre of
many shopping expeditions from people all over Monmouthshire,
although the other market towns of Abergavenny, Chepstow and
Newport also attracted housewives, farmers and housekeepers
from the big houses for all their Christmas shopping. Shops even
catered for the nobility, with a 'silver service' in assistance
which we rarely see today, and a fine selection of quality gift
ideas straight from London and the Continent. It was rarely
necessary – and inconvenient – to travel further afield than
one's county town before the Second World War. In 1934 the
Monmouthshire Beacon *did a most impressive piece to*
advertise the shopping in the county town. Sadly, none of these
old names remains on the shops which now line the shopping
streets yet some had existed there for nigh on two hundred years.

With Christmas close at hand the gift problem is bound to confront many people, and with a view to facilitating their task, a brief reference is made below of some of the attractive displays which are worthy of inspection.

At Lugg & Russels, Christmas gifts of quality are a feature. Those of a discriminating taste will be able to make their choice from a varied selection of handkerchiefs, blouses, jumpers, suits, silk underwear, dressing gowns and other things to wear. A representative collection of 'Jaeger' products

are also displayed, and there is no doubt that those who are fortunate enough to receive a gift purchased from this leading establishment will possess the very best of its kind.

Frost, Southwick Ltd of Church Street cater for everyone by presenting presents at a wide range of prices. Among these we must mention mirrors, brushes, powderbowls and puffs, perfumes (at competitive prices) and other presents to suit both sexes.

FOR THE LADIES With the usual rush of social engagements, ladies will turn to permanent waving, and Mr H.H. Keeling of 48 Monnow Street has fully qualified operators in charge of this process. Various methods are incorporated and the scale of charges is moderate. A guarantee of satisfaction is a factor that should be noted.

The thirty departments of London House, Newport combine in displaying a wonderful range of novelties which make the gift problem simple of solution. The Toytown has been visited by thousands of kiddies, and parents will receive the utmost help when selecting their gifts at this popular store.

The old established house of Lewis & James again offers seasonable presents in all departments. In the fancy department tunic shirts, night shirts, pyjamas, tie and scarf sets, gloves, and collars and hats are all on display. Indoor and outdoor footwear are a feature of the boot department, while male attire is represented by overcoats, raincoats, suits, sports coats, leather coats, etc.

THINGS TO EAT The Christmas Show at William Hall & Co's, Agincourt Square, includes a selection of crackers, fruits, fancy biscuits, chocolates, iced cakes, wines and other provisions. Novelties of all kinds are also included and the housewife has no difficulty choosing all the good things to eat and drink that are associated with this season.

The injunction from J.S. Gower, Draper, Monnow Street, to 'Shop early', has met with great response, and the inexpensive and useful presents shown by this house have a general appeal. Popular lines are fancy cloths, bedspreads, quilts, cushions, old bleached linens, underwear, cardigans, jumpers and tea cosies.

Books are always popular and the difficulty of selecting the right ones will soon appear on a visit to C.H. Howse, The Library, Agincourt Square. Here a wide and various stock of popular literature can be inspected at leisure and both young and old have been thought of in its display.

Harry Hill, of Agincourt Square, invites shoppers to view his selection of perfumes, toilet requisites, cameras. A popular gift, and one which is certain to be appreciated, is a calendar with a postcard enlargement of the given's favourite snapshot. His attractively dressed windows contain many helpful suggestions.

Williams, Cotton & Co., have established a reputation for high-class Christmas provisions and a glance at their announcement elsewhere in this issue shows that they are again ready to help the housewife. A speciality is puff pastry and almond paste, both ready for use. Christmas cakes are another product recommended for consideration by this firm who also stock the best brands of wines and spirits.

'Halls' gifts are sure to please' is a slogan that has become well known locally, and their windows in Monnow Street are attractively dressed with ladies' dance frocks and a range of ladies' gifts at extremely reasonable prices. The question of 'What shall I give?' can be easily solved by visiting these premises.

What could be nicer for a Christmas gift than a smart piece of jewellery? For an extensive selection of articles of this kind, and also watches, leather goods, and wedding and engagement rings, a visit to Messrs Badman & Co., of Monmouth and of Coleford, is recommended.

ALL THE BEST The name of Sterret is associated with cakes of distinctive design and excellence of quality. This year they are again offering all that is best in Christmas fare, and a Christmas cake supplied by this firm satisfies the most exacting connoisseur of Christmas eatables.

A special show of afternoon and dance frocks is included at the Bon Marche in Church Street. There is a large variety of new goods to choose from . . .

'The Old Firm', as L. Hunt's establishment is known, offers all the leading makes in cycles, motor-cycles and radio. A bicycle is often every schoolboy's desire, and his wishes can easily be fulfilled by a visit to this store.

No Christmas would be real Christmas if the fare were not of the best quality. B. Partridge of the Central Stores stresses the high quality of his groceries; and Christmas cakes and mince pies are only two of the many lines that deserve special notice.

The children will find toys after their own heart at Smith's Bargain Stores, 86, Monnow Street. Inspection is welcomed.

All the drinks in demand at Christmas time will be available from C.N. Ballinger, Glendower Street. For wishing friends a Merry Christmas and to drink their health a good stock is of paramount importance and those can be delivered to your door in convenient quantities.

A photograph forms an intimate gift for Christmas or New Year, and Mr E.H. de Heanman of St James Square specializes in supplying presents of this character . . .

Personal attention is given at Pitman's Stores, Whitecross Street, where special Christmas goods are on show. Crackers, Scotch shortbread, and all the other good things to eat can be purchased.

The windows of W. Marsh, Church Street, have an admirable attraction for young folk as well as old. Meccano and Hornby trains are a speciality among the range of toys,

games and novelties which should enable all parents to act 'Father Christmas' with great success.

The feature goes on at great length to include, with true Christmas charity, every merchant within the area, from the coal and log merchants to the smaller and less attractive shops, opticians, gas installers and car battery sales. Christmas was much more practical in those days!

Superstitions and Sayings

Every region has its own sayings and beliefs which develop as a result of the weather and land lore and peculiarities of the area. Here are a few from Monmouthshire. Many are related to apple trees, as the north-eastern borders of the county merge into Herefordshire, both counties having a strong tradition for cider and perry.

Beat the trees on Christmas night and they will bear more fruit.

If you tie wet bands of straw around the trunks of the trees in the orchard on Christmas Eve, they will become more fruitful.

A Monmouthshire Christmas

Sunshine sunfire on Christmas Day
Means fires throughout the coming year.

If sun shines on the fruit trees on Christmas Day, they will
bear well at harvest time.

Put a stone on the fruit trees in your orchard on Christmas
Eve, this will ensure a heavy harvest of fruit.

Purify your fields with the smoke of a burning hawthorn bush
on Christmas night and ensure a healthy crop. [See 'Boro
Divvus', p. 50 above]

Give back to the tree some of its juice, and it will thank thee
with a bountiful crop. [This refers to wassailing]

A windy Christmas, a good crop of apples.

When it snows they say the Welshmen are plucking their
geese.

If the birds sing before Candlemas they will cry before May.
[Candlemas is 2 February]

The robin and the wren are God's Christmas gifts to men.
The swallow and the swifts are God's New Year gifts.

If Christmas Day be bright and clear
There will be two winters in the year.

Turkey Patrol

In the hard years after the Second World War, poultry rustling was rife in Monmouthshire just before Christmas. This account from the Monmouthshire Beacon *describes how the Monmouthshire constabulary tackled the matter in December 1950.*

The scheme devised by the Chief Constable of Monmouthshire, Mr Ronald Alderson, to protect Christmas poultry from 'rustlers' paid good dividends.

At only six isolated places in the county were the rustlers successful – only 33 chickens, 2 geese and 2 turkeys were stolen.

That total represented an infinitesimal percentage of the number of birds which found their way to the Christmas dinner tables.

It also speaks highly for the efficiency of the police officers who manned the cars comprising the 'Turkey Patrol', officers who, throughout the hours of darkness, kept watch on the 295 farms and smallholdings in the area.

Some of the farms had as many as 8,000 head of poultry (about £50,000 worth) ready for the Christmas market; others had stocks of 2,000–3,000 birds.

After midnight, all vehicles seen were checked by the patrol, and there were two instances of court cases.

A policeman cycling along a road at High Cross, Rogerstone, at 3 a.m. one day, heard a disturbance among some chickens. He investigated and found three hens had been killed. Searching for the culprit with his flashlight, he saw him making away at speed – a fox! There was no arrest.

During the recent icy spell, the snow-packed roads caused many accidents and the patrol proved invaluable, in some cases rendering first aid and other help. The experienced police drivers in the patrol did not have one accident, though conditions were bad.

The 'Turkey Patrol' may have ended their work, but every night radio cars still patrol the county's roads.

In Case of Fire, Throw Carol Singer in Brook!

JUDITH RUSSILL

Judith Russill is a naturally inquisitive lady. Although she was not born in Tintern, everybody at the Abbey information centre and the local hotels refers to her as 'Tintern's archivist'. It is often surprising to discover exactly how much a late arrival such as Judith can discover about her adopted home. Here she supplies a few snippets of information about Christmas in one of Monmouthshire's most beautiful locations.

The Wye Valley, and Tintern in particular, are best remembered as the inspiration of poets, and the birthplace of the picturesque,

when young gentlemen of quality were prevented from enjoying 'The Grand Tour', by the Napoleonic Wars.

What is less well known is that the whole valley was an industrial area, the birthplace of the wire industry in the sixteenth century, black with soot, the night sky lit by the glare of furnaces, and most important for any historical researcher. It had a transient and highly mobile population: that fact alone causes major headaches when it comes to tracing particular customs or families.

There was a tendency for incomers to bring their own customs with them. A good case in point is the Welsh custom of Calennig, giving a decorated apple for Christmas luck. Locally they called it 'Monty'. The question is: was it here all the while, or did Welsh industrial workers bring it with them a few centuries ago?

What I can say with confidence is that good works have endured in the village, surviving the departure of any family.

Tintern is richly endowed with Christmas doles of various types. There is one that gives a food parcel without discrimination to anyone who needs it. It usually consists of soup, jars of jam, etc. – not to any great value, but useful nevertheless.

The Chapel Hill United Charity was formed in 1910 from the amalgamation of three earlier charities, the oldest dating from 1634. This Christmas charity now provides a voucher worth in the region of £10–£12 to be spent at any of the village stores. It is awarded to the pensioners of the parish.

The charity board is a bit like the Academie Française: when somebody dies or moves away, a new member is appointed. In such a way these charities have survived the complete changeovers of population that this area has seen every few decades.

This has spawned a general desire to match the efforts of

An open-air carol service held in the picturesque ruins of Tintern Abbey, 1981.

older generations at Christmas time with new initiatives. One of the most recent is the carol service in the ruins of Tintern Abbey. The Revd Arnott has been the guiding light here. The money raised goes to Barnados.

Organized carol singing is very popular now. A few years ago, a party of carol singers was progressing round by candlelight on one gusty evening, when one poor soul ignited herself with her candle! She promptly repaired to a local brook, where the fire was eventually extinguished without major injury.

A number of people round here used to go over to the Clay family, who lived near St Arvans. Before Christmas they would give a sherry party in aid of charity. You really had to be in the know, as it was quite easy to get lost trying to find the house if you were a recent arrival in the village.

I have tried to find out more about calendar customs around Tintern without much success. I think that part of the problem is that before the war you tended to work locally alongside old Ifor, who would do something different, and obviously you would find out why. That way the knowledge survived Ifor's departure.

Now the situation is different. Few work locally. Most people commute, so the knowledge is not handed on. I have found villagers even ignorant about local place-names!

I don't honestly believe that Tintern could be regarded as Welsh in any real sense of the word. It probably hasn't been that way for centuries. It is sad really to think that there has not been any real continuity of Christmas custom since the days of the abbey, but then the population was scattered to the four winds.

A Showman's Christmas

HENRY DANTER

Henry Danter is the sometimes controversial owner of the fairground at Symonds Yat West, less than two miles from the Welsh border. Generations of Welshmen and others have flocked

A Monmouthshire Christmas

across from Monmouthshire to enjoy the holiday atmosphere of a day out, at what has been a traditional site for a cross-border fairground. This is his account of what showpeople across the whole of South Wales did at Christmas time in the 1950s and '60s.

The weather was often against open-air fairgrounds in Gwent and south-east Wales at Christmas time. We often had the right to pitch at different sites in Abergavenny and Newport among others, but by the 1950s not many of them were used. Most families would be heading for over-winter sites in Gloucestershire or Hereford.

When I was a boy long slow-moving convoys would be seen being towed by lorries or tractors along the Heads of the Valleys Road, or the Newport–Monmouth Road.

Older folks told me that it was much slower in the days of horses and traction engines before the war, and they often had to stay overnight in a farmer's field, while the horses were watered or the traction engines stoked up. Even when I was a lad, getting to the winter site near Ross-on-Wye could mean an overnight stop on the way up, before the dual carriageway was built to Monmouth in the 1960s.

The best Christmas fair was held under the shelter of the old iron bridge at Merthyr Tydfil. It didn't go on for very long – usually three days. Sometimes the showmen would pack up early if the takings were poor, and they would take the Heads of the Valleys Road past Brynmawr and down into Abergavenny. Whole families would travel with the fair, and the kids would get very fed up being in a van or lorry cab all the time when it was raining outside. It wasn't easy for the mothers.

The kids would help out on the stalls, trying to get their own sales pitch going. Often you would see during working days kids who should have been at school, working the stalls, trying to get extra money for Christmas. Everyone was trying

to put money away against the long winter stretch when there would be no fairs until Easter.

Some of the men would spend Christmas drinking their profits, others would go down to Newport to try and pick up a new van or generator going cheap. Winter was also the time for buying in new rides; sometimes they were bought new, while some might try and pick up a second-hand ride from Barry Island or Porthcawl.

The families always stuck together. Even if you spent half your time fighting with each other, if anyone had some bad luck, then we would all help. Christmas was a time for meeting up and deciding what to do. Some families would plan, others would suddenly make a decision to go somewhere else next year, in the hope of making more money.

We always had a Christmas party. Everyone would put some money up for the kids at Christmas. A lot of the stuff would be bought, as I don't think cooking was easy on caravan stoves when you had been on the move for most of the year. The mothers always saw to it, the men had other things to do. The party was always very noisy, with the kids getting excited, blowing squeakers, sometimes fighting over pieces of cake, wearing funny hats, pulling crackers and everyone talking at once.

The men would have a race for a bottle. One year we were camped with several other families near Ross-on-Wye, and we raced round the town. I was quite young, and I came in first, so I won a bottle of whisky. I had never drunk whisky before, so I tried to show off by drinking it all in one go. It nearly killed me!

A Memory

IDRIS DAVIES

When Christmastide to Rhymney came
And I was six or seven,
I thought the stars in the eastern skies
Were the brightest stars of heaven.

I chose the star that glittered most
To the east of Rhymney town
To be the star above the byre
Where Mary's babe lay down.

And nineteen hundred years would meet
Beneath a magic light,
And Rhymney share with Bethlehem
A star on Christmas night.

Dreaming of an
Arctic Christmas?

The Christmas of 1962/3 stands out for the terrible weather conditions, Christmas holidays spent digging sheep out of drifts, food wasted as expected house guests did not make it through the snow, children's memories of no school and tobogganing all day. New Year's Day heralded more bad news, as the New Year issue of the Monmouthshire Beacon *relates.*

ARCTIC WEATHER PERSISTS – CHAOTIC CONDITIONS IN MONMOUTH DISTRICT – HUGE SNOWDRIFTS BLOCK ROADS – ONE BRIGHT SPOT – NO ACCIDENTS!

Huge snowdrifts, over ten feet deep, blocked many roads in the Monmouthshire rural area as a result of the blizzard which swept the district in the early hours of Sunday morning. Traffic was seriously disrupted and a number of villages were cut off.

On Tuesday morning there was no sign of a change in the arctic weather and the forecast was for more snow. Another blizzard hit the district during Wednesday night and with more snow on Thursday, conditions were as bad as ever.

The town and countryside is covered with a heavy blanket of snow, and conditions are reminiscent of those experienced in early 1947.

People in the rural areas have been faced with the problem of obtaining supplies and many stranded villagers have had to

Snow over Bedwelly and Tredegar.

go long distances, either on foot or by tractor, across snow-covered fields to fetch food.

Farmers are experiencing many difficulties, particularly where milk supplies have to be got away, and motorists still face hazardous conditions, yet no accidents have been reported.

Apart from the demand for bread and food supplies and footwear, business in the towns this week has been slack, but a number of shops have been short of staff due to some employees, living in the rural areas, being unable to reach town. On Monday (23rd) one man was determined to get to his work and proceeded part of the way on horseback from Trellech as far as The Gockett where the road was blocked by drifts.

Road conditions on Sunday were so bad that no buses left the Red and White depot at Monmouth, but on Monday services were operating to Newport, Gloucester, Lydney and through the Wye Valley to Chepstow. The service through to Hereford could not run because of the road being blocked at Welsh Newton and St Weonards.

Traffic in the town has been much lighter than usual and more tractors than ever have been seen in the streets, many coming from the country districts to collect essential supplies. On Tuesday (Christmas Eve) two Monmouth grocery firms made use of a tractor and a Land-rover to deliver to customers in the Maypole and Newcastle areas, which were cut off.

Postal deliveries and collections, particularly in the rural areas, have presented no easy task for postmen and mail-van drivers, yet they have failed to reach only a few areas.

County council roadmen have had a busy time with snowploughs and mechanical scoops.

Tobogganing has been popular among children, but some young people in Wyesham had the novel idea of building an igloo!

BLOWN INTO HOUSES About six inches of snow fell on Sunday morning (29th), and the high wind not only swept it into drifts but even through doors and windows of houses. It also found its way under roofs and many people had the unexpected job of carrying bucketsful of snow down from the lofts to prevent damage to the ceilings. Drifts had to be cleared from outside most houses.

Early on Monday morning a Red and White bus conveying workmen from Monmouth to the Royal Ordnance factory at Dinham, only managed to get as far as Lydart where it ran into a drift.

The driver, Mr Norman Reynolds told a *Beacon* reporter that it was over ten feet deep. 'I had no alternative but to

An igloo was one way of keeping warm! This one was built in
Bedwelly, 1972

abandon my bus and dig through the drift so that the
passengers could get out. The snow was blowing off the field
furiously and it was so cold it froze on my coat and hat,' he
said. Another bus was sent from the depot to bring the
workmen back to town.

Llanishen has suffered severely through snowdrifts which
blocked all roads into the village. However, on Sunday one
farmer, Mr Peter Davies, had to get his milk to a Chepstow
dairy. Driving a tractor he eventually got through a drift and
succeeded in delivering his milk.

However, the wind and snow on Sunday caused further
drifting and villagers became anxious as they had had no
bread deliveries since Friday. But on Monday morning a van
conveying supplies managed to travel along the Trellech road

as far as Hygga Farm, where a snowplough had been at work. From that spot the bread had to be carried by people from the village but they were only too thankful that it had been brought so far.

Despite the weather, Monmouth Market was held on Monday, and the few stock that did arrive were in keen demand and sold well.

During Monday night and on New Year's Day, there was more snow, and with further falls during Wednesday and Thursday, the outlook was very grim. Traffic was unable to negotiate Whitchurch Pitch with the result that newspapers were three hours late reaching Monmouth. The telephone exchange has been extremely busy this week and at peak times people have been asked to restrict their calls to three minutes.

Mr W.S. Hall, the local manager of James and Emanuel Coal Merchants, told the *Beacon* that they were doing all they could to supply as many people in the town with coal. They were being hampered by the road conditions, and many people were fetching supplies in their cars and other vehicles.

Naturally many people are becoming anxious as to the possibility of flooding when the thaw comes, but much will depend on whether it is accompanied by heavy rain.

A QUIET WELCOME FOR THE NEW YEAR Many people stayed indoors around their own firesides to welcome in the New Year.

Owing to the bad weather, the Monmouthshire Hunt ball, which was to have been held at the Beaufort Arms Hotel, Monmouth, and the British Legion dance at the Rolls Hall were cancelled, while the bells of St Mary's Priory Church did not ring to welcome the New Year, owing to the lack of ringers.

However, during the night someone had the right spirit and wished everyone the compliments of the season in a novel

way by pressing snow on to the garden wall of St Bride's, The Parade, wishing everyone, 'A Happy New Year' in large letters.

Unfortunately the weather prevented the traditional New Year's Day meet of Monmouthshire Hounds in Agincourt Square, for the second year running.

from

Diary of a Farmer's Wife – 2

MARY ANNE HUGHES

This second extract from the Diary *describes further merrymaking in the Hughes household.*

Dec. ye 27. Christmas be all over now, and our visitors gone, but a right good time did we have, the roads did dry up a bit so not so bad for the travellers, who did cum pack horse. Cusson Tom and Emma, her lad and his sweetheart, Jan, did get here after a journie of hard going Christmas Eve, the rest did cum Christmas morning and all of us to church leaving carters wiffe and Sarahs sister Jane to help Sarah with the dinner to be all ready genst our cumming back, and mother

and me did set the tables together in a row and cover them with my linnen table cloths; then we did put the silver and glass and all did look verrie fine. Passon did give a verrie good sermon, telling us to do to others as we would have them do to us, and the world the better place, to which I do agree. The singing did go right heartilie with a great roar, and the church bein full, for all do like the young passon and his mother.

Then we went out and home to our dinner. John did set at one end with the beef and geese, and farmer Ellis at the other to cut up the hams and so on, which Sarah and Jane did carry round till all served, and all did eat their fill and had plentie. Then John did pass the wine and all did drink each others healths; then the men did smoke while we ladies did drink our wine and talk of divers things that had happened through the year, not thinking so much had; then the men did say let us dance, so Bill and Jan did play a merrie jig on their fiddles and we did step it out finely; till all breathless we did sit down laffing much.

Farmer Bliss did say lets have a story so Passon did tell us a good one that did cause much merriement; then John did say he would tell them the story of what happened when his father died, and did tell of the man who stopped him on the road. His mother did say it must have bin Joe Graves who did go to them for shelter when in trouble, and they did hide him for three days and he getting off safe at last. Then said Mistress Prue it showed how one good turn did make another.

Then cusson Tom saying we be getting too serious, so Mistress Prue to the spinette to play a merrie tune, and we to dancing once more stepping it right merrilie till Sarah do say its time for tea; whereupon we do sit down and do justice to all the good things provided, which did make a brave show and looked verrie good on the dishes; the lights from the tapers in Johns mothers silver candle sticks did light the holly

Sarah had put on the table in glasses. All the ladies did like mothers meat cake, and want to know how to make it.

Then we did gather together and play the game of Popp; we did put the chairs in a ringe, the men on one side, the ladies on the other with our hands behind, one holding a apple which be passed from one to another. The man must not speak but do beckon to the lady they think have got the apple, if she have not she do say 'popp', and the man do have to sit on the floor and pay forfitt, till all there; but if he be right he do take the lady on his knees till the game be played out. After we did play bobbie apple, and snap draggon, the Passon burning his fingers mitilie to get Sarahs plum; all did enjoy it much, and then we did stop awhile for sume cakes and wine, and sum songs sung by one and other; then more dancing till supper, then more games and later all home after a really good Christmas which we did all enjoy much with everybody happie. And now this be the last page in my little book. I do not know if I shall ever write another one. I do feel I have much to be thankful for, for my life with John and his mother be a verrie happy one.

I do wonder where my little book will go, who may read it. I shall always keep it and perhaps if God do give me a son he will read it someday and so know what a fine man his father is. So I say goodby to my little book.

When Newspaper Editors were Men of Goodwill!

The Monmouthshire Beacon *began in the 1830s and still runs today. In its heyday it regaled its readers with a society column, news from abroad and everything one expects of a good national daily. Here, in the issue dated 26 December 1840, its editor writes his Christmas message to his readers with as much aplomb as a royal speech. What he wrote 150 years ago is as valid today and thus serves as a fitting epitaph for the Monmouthshire Christmas.*

All connections between us and our readers must have ceased 'ere we forego the good old fashion of congratulating them on each return of the 'Great Festival'. None we think should be more ready than the Journalist to give the 'All Hail' on those happy occasions, as none can boast of a larger circle of acquaintance: and though he may reckon among his friends many whose faces he has never seen, between them and him there yet exists an understood intimacy; he has, through the whole year, been trying to cultivate their good opinion – their gossip, their adviser, their confidant, their advocate – their table companion, a favoured inmate of the family, admitted to the board, received at the hearth. And though the number of his anxious and exciting duties allow but little leisure for the

Santa travels to Monmouth by pony trap and by boat.

outward show of courtesy, he is not the less mindful or grateful as annually he embraces the opportunity of wishing them, with all his heart, a 'MERRY CHRISTMAS'.

Society, manners and customs have changed and with them Christmas too. It is no longer observed as it once was, when in cot and castle the holly and the mistletoe stood for weeks together, and the loud laugh and the joyous gambol, the merry mask and mumming, echoed from, and were acted under, every English rooftree, when the 'heir with the roses in his shoes' mingled with hardy retainers, happy as himself, and old jests and old ale flowed with equal freedom.

Yet Christmas 'is merry Christmas still': a season of jovial feasting, and the interchange of good feeling and good fellowship – a season to which, from old custom and habit, we are wont to look forward with pleasure and expectation, during those short and dreary winter days when 'the rain and the wind beat dark December' – a season whose unimportant but innocent and cheerful associations brighten the heart, as its great festive log does the hearth, gladdening youth and recalling to the recollection of old age so many bygone Christmases at once, along which, as along a line of beacon fires that lighten the view and lead the eye, it may look far back even to earliest infancy.

It is eminently the festival of England; and whether at home or abroad, there are few of her sons who forget its observances. In reading one of the three great Arctic Expeditions, we were struck with an interesting entry, describing the manner in which Christmas Day was kept in that dreary region, amid a wild and trackless waste of frozen waters, by the hardy crew, who then seemed to derive no small degree of solace and comfort from the feeling that, though far, far away from their loved homes in merry England, they could still enjoy some communion with their distant countrymen, in celebrating the same happy day, so

far as their scanty means would allow, in the same happy manner.

If amid those majestic solitudes, the most awfully sublime scenes of nature, the tenants of two adventurous voyage-worn barks could forget the vast space which separated them from their friends, their danger and sufferings, the desolate prospects around them, in the enjoyment of those pleasing recollections and associations which the day recalled, old Christmas must not be cast aside as an obsolete folly without its use or advantage. While England retains her old feelings, she retains her old festivals: the love of country is but a sentiment made up of innumerable such small attachments — like the little threads that compose the cable, and by withdrawing of any we weaken the whole. May it continue forever, then, and our friends live long to observe it, and keep us company through life; the waif is carried with the waters, and as they advance so we hope to progress.

The year now drawing to its end like the pages of the volume we will shortly close, is chequered over with passages of bright and dark, joy and sadness, life's excitements and death's triumphs; the marriage procession and the funeral train; the bride and the mourner have crossed its track: and we are now looking back on the wreck of an old year, and preparing to begin a new one, whose womb is doubtless as full of startling events and strange occurrences. But about those, whatever they may be, it is useless to fret now.

We do not ask our readers to look grave: let them smile, and be as happy and merry as we can wish them, as the week

> Brings Bly the Christmas back again
> With all his hospitable train.

Acknowledgements

All unattributed work is by Maria von Staufer, using published and unpublished reference material and personal interviews. Acknowledgement and sincere thanks goes to all those who have helped with research material and personal memories, drawings and general running around, especially Fr Smith, and Phillip and Elizabeth Alcock of St Mary's Catholic Church, Monmouth; the Keeper at Tredegar House, Newport for all the help and permission to go through the Morgan family papers; Monmouth Museum for use of their resource material; Monmouth Library for all their advice and assistance; Chepstow Library; John Bevan for his help with The Rucusants' Christmas'; Robin Gwyndaf for his helpful assistance and advice; Roy Saer for the use of his material in the piece 'Plygain'; both curators of the Museum of Welsh Life, Cardiff; the editor and staff of the *South Wales Argus*, particularly for their assistance by publishing my request for memories, and generously permitting use of their material; Mr G. Bartlett of the National Meteorological Library; Mrs Judith Russill, Tintern Archivist; the *Abergavenny Gazette* for allowing us to pour over their archives; the editor and staff of the *Monmouthshire Beacon* for their friendly assistance, generosity and encouragement; Mrs Joyce Edmonds for permission to use her books, *Tales of the Llanishen Parishes* and *Tales of Old St Arvans*, for the material in 'Carolling Gaily' and 'Christmas in St Arvans'; the *South Wales Argus* for permission to reprint part of 'The Calennig' and 'Abergavenny's Magi', both by Fred Hando, and also readers' Christmas memories in the piece 'I Remember a Christmas . . .'; Penguin Books Ltd for permission to print the Christmas extracts from *Diary of a Farmer's Wife* (Allen Lane, 1980, first published in *Farmers' Weekly* © Mollie Preston, 1937, 1964, 1980); Marijan Hubert for permission to use his poem, 'Memories of Christmas', published in the Taliesin Poetry Book, 1994, entitled *Out of Hearing*; the Society of Nativitists for permission to reproduce the article 'Christmas in a Welsh Vicarage' from their *Journal*, Christmas 1987; the *Monmouthshire Beacon* for the use of their material throughout this book, especially, 'Dreaming of an Arctic Christmas?', 'The Grand Christmas Stock Show' and 'Turkey

Patrol'; the Historical Society of the Church in Wales for 'Plygain', part of an article entitled 'Y Plygain', by Gwynfryn Richards, from their society journal, 1947; Mrs Rosalind Gardiner of Kingfisher Cruises for her help with identifying the players in the Whitchurch Pantomime. However hard we tried, there remain a small number of elusive sources which we have not been able to trace. To these gentle authors and artists we humbly offer the inclusion of their works in this book as a small tribute to the artistic and literary names of Monmouthshire.

Picture Credits

The *South Wales Argus*, pp. 54, 81, 98, 106, 131, 137 and 139; the Museum of Welsh Life, pp. 11, 12 and 17; Tredegar House, pp. 29, 30 and 32; the *Monmouthshire Beacon*, p. 39; Monmouth Nelson Museum, p. 84; Kingfisher Cruises, Symonds Yat, p. 114; Tegwyn Roberts, p. 17; all other illustrations are from the authors' collection.